Spreading the Fire

Book 1, Acts 1–8

The
ACTS
of the
HOLY
SPIRIT
Series

BOOK
1

Spreading the Fire

A New Look at
Acts — God's
Training Manual
for Every Christian

C. PETER WAGNER

Regal Books
A Division of Gospel Light
Ventura, California, U.S.A.

Published by Regal Books
A Division of Gospel Light
Ventura, California, U.S.A.
Printed in U.S.A.

Regal Books is a ministry of Gospel Light, an evangelical Christian publisher dedicated to serving the local church. We believe God's vision for Gospel Light is to provide church leaders with biblical, user-friendly materials that will help them evangelize, disciple and minister to children, youth and families.

It is our prayer that this Regal Book will help you discover biblical truth for your own life and help you meet the needs of others. May God richly bless you.

For a free catalog of resources from Regal Books/Gospel Light please contact your Christian supplier or call 1-800-4-GOSPEL.

Scripture quotations in this publication are from the *New King James Version*. Copyright © 1979, 1980, 1982 Thomas Nelson, Inc. Used by permission.

Verses marked (*TLB*) are taken from *The Living Bible* © 1971. Used by permission of Tyndale House Publishers, Inc., Wheaton, IL 60189. All rights reserved.

Note: Italicized words and phrases in Scripture quotations throughout the book are added by the author for emphasis and clarification.

This book is also available in Spanish (ISBN 1-56063-846-X) and Portuguese (1-56063-942-3). Published by Editorial Unilit, Miami, FL.

Library of Congress Cataloging-in-Publication Data

Wagner, C. Peter.
    A modern commentary on Acts / C. Peter Wagner.
        p. cm.
    Contents: v. 1. Spreading the fire : Acts 1—8
    ISBN 0-8307-1711-0 (v. 1)
    1. Bible. N.T. Acts—Commentaries. I. Title.
BS2625.3.W35 1994
226.6'07—dc20
                                                        94-30400
                                                            CIP

10 9 8 7 6 5 4 3 2 1 / KP / 99 98 97 96 95 94

Rights for publishing this book in other languages are contracted by Gospel Literature International (GLINT). GLINT also provides technical help for the adaptation, translation and publishing of Bible study resources and books in scores of languages worldwide. For further information, contact GLINT, P.O. Box 4060, Ontario, CA 91761-1003, U.S.A., or the publisher.

Contents

Introduction

This commentary on the book of Acts is my first attempt at a verse-by-verse exposition of a book of the Bible. It may be the last. As a field missionary and a professional missiologist, I have been consumed by the Acts of the Apostles, which I regard as a kind of owner's manual for implementing the Great Commission. I have studied and taught Acts more than any other book.

The full rationale for choosing to undertake this massive project is so crucial to understanding Acts as a whole, that I begin the first book of this series with a whole chapter to explain it.

Because I am not known in the academic world as a biblical scholar, I have asked my friend Professor Russell P. Spittler, who is so known, to peruse the manuscripts previous to publication and to monitor the technical elements of biblical scholarship that appear from time to time. This does not imply Dr. Spittler's personal endorsement of each of my *interpretations* of the biblical text. Many of the themes I discuss fall clearly into areas of contemporary theological dialogue and even controversy. So many of them do, in fact, that it may be no reader at all will end up agreeing with everything I say!

Be that as it may, I am deeply indebted to Russ Spittler for his wise and knowledgeable counsel, as well as to the several authors of standard commentaries on Acts whom I frequently quote.

C. Peter Wagner
Fuller Theological Seminary
Pasadena, California

God's Training Manual for Modern Christians

Many modern Christians are not satisfied with Christianity as usual. They are fed up with playing church. The status quo has little appeal. Their desire is to look back at the end of the day or at the end of the year and say, "Praise God! His kingdom has advanced and He has allowed me to be a part of it." They don't want to be spectators, they want to be participants in the great work God is doing today.

For those desiring to be a part of God's action in their churches, their communities and the world out there, nothing will help more than understanding the book of Acts and applying what we can learn from it. Acts was designed to be God's training manual for modern Christians. Seeing what worked so well almost 2,000 years ago will directly apply to our service to God today and can provide a welcome power boost to your Christian life. Your serious study of Acts will bring new intimacy with the Father and new joy in doing His will.

Studying Acts and Living It

Acts has been an important book to me from the beginnings of my Christian life in 1950. On the very day I accepted Jesus Christ as my Lord and Savior, I committed my life to world evangelization. Because I was not raised in a Christian home, when I became a Christian at age 19 I knew virtually nothing of the Christian life and less about Christian ministry. Nevertheless, from the moment I was born again I knew I was going to be a missionary.

By God's grace, my wife, Doris, and I were permitted to spend the first 16 years of our active ministry as field missionaries to Bolivia. Then in 1971 we returned to the United States, where I accepted a position on the faculty of the Fuller Seminary School of World Mission and began my career as a professional missiologist. All of my Christian activities have been centered around obeying Jesus' Great Commission to make disciples of all nations (see Matt. 28:19,20).

Because I was one of those looking for a place on the front lines of God's work in the world, I soon discovered that the book of Acts was written for me. Not only did I spend considerable time in Acts during my personal Bible study, but I also began teaching it whenever I could.

My greatest opportunity for serious study and teaching in Acts came when I participated in founding a new adult Sunday School class in Lake Avenue Congregational Church in Pasadena, California. It was one of almost 30 such adult classes in the church, and I had around 100 adults of all ages who joined me in wanting to be part of something new. The book of Acts was declared our textbook from the outset, and 12 years later, at this writing, we are still drinking from the wells of spiritual water it provides and learning how to apply what we learn to our lives and service for God.

We took our class name, 120 Fellowship, from the band of 120 disciples in the Upper Room reported in Acts 1:15. When we did, we prayed that what had happened to them on the Day of Pentecost, and afterward, would also happen to us. By God's grace, to some degree at least, it has. We certainly are not where we eventually hope to be, but we are grateful that God has allowed us to move steadily along the road toward our goal. No one has said it better than one of our class leaders, Cathy Schaller, while she was describing our class to the congregation as a whole: "We not only want to study the book of Acts, we want to live it!"

Why Another Commentary on Acts?

Through the years, I have done what scholars are expected to do and built up a library of reference material on Acts. I have acquired commentaries, lives of Paul, lives of Peter, histories of early Christianity, sociological and archaeological studies of the first-century world, expositions of Pauline theology, sermons on Acts and specific applications of Acts to certain areas of ministry such as evangelism, small groups and church growth. Many others have gone before me in deciding that their principal field of biblical research will also be the Acts of the Apostles.

Of the collection of books I have, measuring at the present time 5 feet 2 inches, 16 of the volumes are verse-by-verse commentaries on Acts. The authors of these volumes include household names in the field of New Testament studies: F. F. Bruce, Ernst Haenchen, Everett Harrison, Simon J. Kistemaker, R. C. H. Lenski, Howard Marshall, Johannes Munck, John R. W. Stott and others. To supplement these, the Fuller Seminary McAlister Library catalogues no fewer than 86 commentaries on Acts. Research librarian, Olive Brown, did a computer search and discovered that 1,398 commentaries on Acts are listed.

Why, then, commentary number 1,399?

To clear the air, I do not pretend to be a biblical scholar, as are many of my colleagues at Fuller Seminary. I hold them in the highest esteem. The other day I overheard my friend Leslie Allen comment that he had read every known scholarly work on Ezekiel 18. I asked him how many scholarly works that might include and I was amazed when he told me he had studied more than 150 authors. No wonder Allen has gained the reputation among peers as the top, living expert on Ezekiel. He can probably recite much of Ezekiel 18 in the original Hebrew. The late F. F. Bruce gained a similar reputation for expertise on the book of Acts in his lifetime.

Neither this volume nor the two that follow will approach the biblical scholarship of Allen, Bruce and many others. Not only do I lack their critical and linguistic tools, but I also lack the patience to read what 150 others have to say about one chapter of the Bible. I do read several such scholars, however, and reflect in my own writings what insights I can glean from them in grammar, theology and historical context. I am deeply grateful for their exegesis, and I, as do many others, lean heavily upon it.

But my personal gifts are in other areas. I am an activist. Most of my research in church growth and missiology is field research as opposed to library research. History is vitally important, but I am not as personally interested in the past as I am in the present and future. I keep reminding myself that yesterday ended last night. I am enough of a pragmatist to have drawn a rather steady flow of criticism over the years. My passion is to get the job, in this case fulfilling the Great Commission, done. As a theoretician, I have discovered that the theories I like best are the ones that work!

I am also a communicator. Although I appreciate the complexity of many issues relating to our Christian faith and practice, I see my role as communicating them to the Body of Christ in terms that common people can understand and act upon. This trait also draws its share of criticism, much of it undoubtedly deserved. But one of my worst fears is boring both myself and my students with deep, complicated, accurate material that no one really cares about. This is why I may at times go to the opposite extreme.

The World Is Changing Rapidly

What, then, can an activist and a communicator hope to add to the shelves of solid, biblical scholarship on Acts?

The answer to this lies in the fact that Christianity at the end of the twentieth century is dramatically different from anything that has been seen in the past. Rapid changes in the worlds of science and technology are commonly recognized. Relatively few, however, realize that equally startling changes have recently been taking place in world Christianity. Some of these changes can be traced back to the turn of the last century. Many more changes have entered since the middle of this century. But even more rapid changes have occurred in our own generation, and within the last 10 years. My assignment as a missiologist is to keep informed as much as I can with what God is currently doing around the globe.

My purpose in commentary number 1,399, therefore, is to attempt to apply the eternal truths of the book of Acts to the contemporary situation, something that, obviously, no one who has written about Acts in the past would have been able to do. This does not mean that insights of the past are obsolete. Much of what has been said in the past still applies, and I will draw on it. But questions are being raised in world Christianity today that never entered the minds of commentators of yesteryear.

What might these questions be?

The Two Crucial Issues

As we go through Acts chapter by chapter, I will highlight these questions. But to set the stage, two crucial issues have been subject to more study, innovation and creative application over the past 10 or 20 years than could previously have been imagined. These can be described as follows:

- Issues of *power ministries* characterized by supernatural healings, deliverances, miracles and spiritual warfare, and
- *Missiological issues* involved in the cross-cultural expansion of the Christian faith.

I heard one observer conjecture that we have learned more about missiology and power ministries in this current generation than in all previous generations combined. This may be an overstatement, but, in any case, it highlights a very important contemporary phenomenon, a phenomenon directly related to the central message of the book of Acts.

The Theme of Acts

I agree with Simon Kistemaker, as do many other commentators, that in Acts 1:8, "Luke presents the theme for the entire book."[1]

Let's take a look at the verse:

> **But you shall receive power when the Holy Spirit has come upon you; and you shall be witnesses to Me in Jerusalem, and in all Judea and Samaria, and to the end of the earth (Acts 1:8).**

Very simply, two themes in this statement contain the last recorded words of Jesus spoken on earth: power ministries and missiology. Of the 16 commentaries I am using the most, only

Stanley M. Horton, a Pentecostal, seems to recognize how the power (*dunamis*) would relate to contemporary power ministries, although he does not make a specific application at this juncture.[2] Likewise, only Paul E. Pierson, a professional missiologist, highlights contemporary insights on cross-cultural ministry.[3] This means that, unless I am mistaken, very few of the existing 1,398 commentaries on Acts deal in any depth or with specifically professional expertise with the two major themes of the book. Most commonly, the authors take Acts 1:8 as a chronological table of contents for the book, but not as an all-pervasive warp and woof through which to interpret each one of the subsequent scenarios described by Luke.

It is in these two areas that I feel I can make enough of a contribution to justify adding yet another commentary on Acts to library shelves. I bring a degree of expertise both in power ministries and missiology that few of the biblical scholars who have produced the classical works on Acts could provide. In doing so, I have no illusions of grandeur. The classical works have a well-deserved reputation as classics. Whether my contribution will last more than a generation, or even that long, remains to be seen.

Power Ministries and Missiology

My experience in power ministries comes through the framework of what has been called the Third Wave. This refers to the third wave of the power of the Holy Spirit experienced through the Body of Christ in the twentieth century; the first being the Pentecostal movement starting at the beginning of the century and the second, the charismatic movement dating back to 1960. The Third Wave does not replace the other two, but flows into the same stream of Holy Spirit renewal.

I began to research and write on this phenomenon in the early '70s with my book *Spiritual Power and Church Growth* (Creation

House, 1986), first titled *Look Out! The Pentecostals Are Coming.* I later published *The Third Wave of the Holy Spirit* (Servant Books, 1988) and *How to Have a Healing Ministry in Any Church* (Regal Books, 1988). My more recent research on prayer and spiritual warfare is reported in, what Regal Books calls, "The Prayer Warrior Series": *Warfare Prayer* (1992), *Prayer Shield* (1992), *Breaking Strongholds in Your City* (1993) and *Churches That Pray* (1993). Some 20 years of research, mostly field research, into power ministries have given me a substantial foundation upon which to make contemporary applications of the incidents recorded in the book of Acts.

Likewise, more than 20 years of participation in what some regard as the premier missiological faculty of recent times have allowed me to absorb knowledge from some of the finest minds in the field. My Fuller School of World Mission colleagues and I have all served as professional field missionaries before joining the faculty. We travel constantly to every continent and share our experiences in depth with the others. This is an enviable position, for which I give God all the thanks, allowing me to see some of the dynamics of the spread of the gospel in Acts that others may have missed.

I have shared this autobiographical information so readers will know that some of the interpretations I will suggest for many passages in Acts are based on careful and reasonable assumptions, even if they differ considerably from more classical interpretations of the same passage. I have no intention to prove that others are wrong and I am right. But, in many cases, I will offer some seemingly novel suggestions that at least may merit careful consideration by thoughtful readers. And my hope is that number 1,399 will help spark a fire of the Holy Spirit that will not die until "this gospel of the kingdom will be preached in all the world as a witness to all the nations" (Matt. 24:14).

Why Acts Is in the Bible

Well over half, or 56 percent, of the New Testament is dedicated to explaining the origins and growth of the Christian movement. These are the Gospels and Acts. Another 38 percent deals with the nurture of existing Christians (the Epistles), and Revelation comprises the remaining 6 percent. This clearly shows us that the primary emphasis of the New Testament is directed toward understanding why and how unbelievers can become believers. Communicating the gospel to the lost is the major theme, and the Gospels and Acts are designed to inform us how it did happen in the past and, in most cases, how it should happen today.

The four Gospels, Matthew, Mark, Luke and John, record the beginnings of the Christian movement. They tell us of remarkable church growth. Jesus began His three years of earthly ministry, according to some calculations, in A.D. 27. He attracted 12 disciples plus some other men and women. This group soon grew to 70, according to Luke 10. By the time we get to Acts, 120 are meeting in the Upper Room after Jesus' ascension to heaven (see Acts 1:15). We later read in 1 Corinthians 15:6 that 500 believers saw the risen Christ at once, a number that may be over and above the 120, giving a possible total of 620.

Some may wonder why I referred to this as "remarkable" growth. I have trained thousands of new church planters over the years, and very few of them have started with nothing and seen their church grow to 620 in only three years. In fact, something less than 3 percent of all churches *ever* grow to 620.

The Gospels are foundational. The book of Acts follows the Gospels to show how Christians built on the solid foundation laid by Jesus after He departed from the earth. It is intended to be a paradigm of how the kingdom of God would be spread worldwide through the centuries until Jesus returns. In planning our service to God today, we draw deeply on the Gospels and the later Epistles, but Acts, more than any other book, is our primary training manual.

The book of Acts records another era of spectacular church growth, which I will detail later on. In general, however, some scholars estimate that over the 30-year span of Acts, the Christian movement grew from 120 to 100,000 among Jews alone. If this is the case, the decadal growth rate would figure to be more than 200 percent, an extremely high rate sustained over such a period of time. The total growth rate would be even greater if the Gentiles were added. Therefore, if taken only as a church growth case study, Acts would qualify as a valuable source for discovering principles and procedures of spreading the gospel.

The Epistles comprise 38 percent of the New Testament. These are designed as guides for the nurture of existing Christians and do not particularly focus on reaching the lost for Christ. Interestingly enough, nothing in the Epistles directly admonishes Christians to evangelize their neighbors, even though there are some indications that it was being done and that evangelizing was a commendable thing for Christians to do.

Most of the Epistles were written while the evangelistic ministry of the book of Acts was unfolding. The Epistles of Peter, John and Hebrews are the exceptions, and possibly Paul's pastoral Epistles as well.

Dr. Luke: A World Christian

Luke, whom Paul calls "the beloved physician" (Col. 4:14), wrote the book of Acts. It was the second volume in his two-volume series on the origins and expansion of Christianity. The opening of Luke's Gospel records that to Luke "it seemed good...to write to you an orderly account, most excellent Theophilus" (Luke 1:3). Then the first verse of Acts picks it up by saying, **The former account I made, O Theophilus** (Acts 1:1).

No one seems to know who Theophilus might have been, but the tie between Acts and the Gospel of Luke is evident. F. F. Bruce says that Luke's description of his first volume as "all that Jesus began both to do and teach, until the day he was taken up...until the day when, by the Holy Spirit, he commissioned the apostles whom he had chosen, and charged them to proclaim the gospel [Acts 1:1,2] exactly summarizes the scope of Luke's Gospel."[4] The Gospel of Luke tells what Jesus did, and Acts tells what He expects His followers to do, both then and now.

Luke was well educated and cultured. Biblical scholars agree that he was "a man possessed of remarkable literary skill, with a fine sense of form and a beautiful style."[5] He was exceptionally well qualified to write these two historical books. Edmund Hiebert describes him as "a competent scholar and first-rate literary historian....His work was characterized by comprehensiveness, thoroughness, accuracy, and orderliness."[6]

Above all, it is important to recognize that Luke was what we call today a "world Christian." He was dedicated to spreading Christianity not only in his hometown of Antioch of Syria or in the city where he later may have settled, Philippi, but also to the unreached peoples of the first-century world. Luke is, in fact, the only Gentile writer of the New Testament, or of the whole Bible for that matter. In Acts, he shows how the walls of separation between Jews and Gentiles were broken down and, thus, writes more about true missiology than any other biblical author.

One of the reasons the book of Acts is such a practical book is that Luke was also a field missionary. As we will see, Luke writes several sections of Acts with the first person "we," indicating that he himself may have drawn from his own diary he kept when he was part of Paul's missionary activities (see Acts 16:10-18; 20:5-21 and 27:1—28:16). It does not appear that Luke was a convert of Paul. He enters the picture on Paul's second term at Troas, presumably as a mature Christian worker. Paul indicates that Luke was with him in his letters to the Colossians (see Col. 4:14), to Philemon (see Philem. 24) and to Timothy (see 2 Tim. 4:11). It was likely that Luke was a person of some financial means.

With an author possessing the qualifications of Dr. Luke, it is no surprise that in the Acts of the Apostles we have a book we can characterize as a training manual for modern Christians.

The Kingdom of God on the Big Screen

A major theological framework for understanding the book of Acts is the kingdom of God. Acts starts with the kingdom of God and ends with it. It opens with a description of the ministry of Jesus during the 40 days between His resurrection and His ascension to heaven by saying that Jesus spoke to His apostles **of the things pertaining to the kingdom of God** (Acts 1:3). At the end of the book, we find the apostle Paul under house arrest in Rome, receiving visitors and **preaching the kingdom of God** (Acts 28:31).

What is the kingdom of God?

The kingdom of God is present, first and foremost, wherever Jesus Christ is acknowledged and served as King. It is not a geopolitical territory with recognized boundaries. It could not join the United Nations. It is a Kingdom not *of* this world, but nevertheless it is *in* this world. It is essentially a spiritual Kingdom, but it also has tangible, visible manifestations.

In one sense, the kingdom of God is future. There will be a day when Jesus "delivers the kingdom to God the Father, when He puts an end to all rule and all authority and power. For He must reign till He has put all enemies under His feet. The last enemy that will be destroyed is death" (1 Cor. 15:24-26). As long as death is with us, the future Kingdom has not yet arrived. When it does come, we will see "a new heaven and a new earth" (Rev. 21:1).

Until that day, we live in a world where many enemies of God and of His people are still present. Satan, the supreme enemy, is spoken of as "the god of this age" (2 Cor. 4:4). John affirms that "the whole world lies under the sway of the wicked one" (1 John 5:19). The devil is known as "the prince of the power of the air" (Eph. 2:2). This language must not be taken lightly. It is used of Satan by those writing on this side of the Cross and the Resurrection. Before Jesus came, things were even worse!

Whereas, in Old Testament times, bright reflections of God's kingdom were seen from time to time, Satan's control, apart from the small segment of humanity descended from Abraham, was almost total. This world never rightfully belonged to Satan, but to its Creator. "The earth is the Lord's, and all its fullness, the world and those who dwell therein" (Ps. 24:1).

Nevertheless, as a result of the strongholds provided through the fall of Adam and Eve into sin, Satan succeeded in usurping power and control of most human beings and of social institutions. He had become so powerful that in the temptation he could offer Jesus the kingdoms of this world, claiming that "this has been delivered to me, and I give it to whomever I wish" (Luke 4:6). This would have included the Egyptians, the Pygmies, the Mayans and Mongols, the Arabs, the Chinese and thousands of other people groups. Interestingly enough, Jesus never denied that Satan actually had such power. In fact, if Satan did not have control of the kingdoms, the temptation would have been a farce. No wonder Jesus would later call him "the ruler of this world" (John 12:31).

Jesus Invades Satan's Kingdom

The situation changed radically through Jesus' life, death and resurrection. When Jesus first came, John the Baptist declared, "The kingdom of heaven is at hand!" (Matt. 3:2). Jesus was also accustomed to "preaching the gospel of the kingdom" (Matt.

4:23), and He later sent out His disciples to "preach, saying, 'The kingdom of heaven is at hand'" (Matt. 10:7). These statements amounted to a declaration of war. Satan's kingdom, referred to in Matthew 12:26, had existed up to that time virtually unthreatened. No longer! Jesus' purpose in coming to earth was clear: "The Son of God was manifested, that He might destroy the works of the devil" (1 John 3:8). The kingdom of God had invaded the kingdom of the enemy.

Much to Satan's dismay, Jesus' death on the cross sealed His ultimate victory over the realm of darkness and assured the world that God's kingdom would continue to expand until the day it would arrive in all fullness and perfection. His death "disarmed principalities and powers" and "made a public spectacle of them, triumphing over them in it" (Col. 2:15).

The radical difference between New Testament times and Old Testament times is described clearly by Jesus' reference to John the Baptist. Jesus affirmed that no greater was born of women than John the Baptist. But John symbolized the ending of the Old Testament age, and Jesus said, "He who is least in the kingdom of heaven is greater than he" (Matt. 11:11). Right afterward, Jesus announced His declaration of war. He said that from the days of John the Baptist, the Kingdom of heaven comes with violence "and the violent take it by force" (Matt. 11:12). By this, Jesus was establishing the pattern of things to come. His people would be recruited, mobilized and empowered to move with force against Satan and on behalf of the kingdom of God.

Spiritual Warfare

The weapons to conduct this spiritual warfare would be spiritual, not carnal. In the Lord's Prayer, Jesus taught His disciples to pray daily, "Your kingdom come. Your will be done on earth as it is in heaven" (Matt. 6:10). He said, "My kingdom is not of this world" (John 18:36).

What would Jesus' kingdom look like? At the outset of His public ministry, Jesus went into the synagogue of his hometown of Nazareth and answered this question. Quoting Isaiah 61, he said He had come to:

- Preach the gospel to the poor;
- Heal the brokenhearted;
- Preach deliverance to the captives;
- Preach recovery of sight to the blind;
- Set at liberty those who are oppressed;
- Preach the acceptable year of the Lord (Luke 4:18,19).

Satan and his kingdom receive a setback every time a sick person is healed, every time a demon is cast out, every time a lost soul is saved, every time a variety of races live together in love and harmony, every time greed is exposed and punished, every time families maintain standards of holiness and purity. Satan, the thief, comes "to steal, and to kill, and to destroy"; but Jesus comes "that they may have life, and that they may have it more abundantly" (John 10:10).

When Jesus left the earth, He left the extension of His kingdom in the hands of His followers empowered by the Holy Spirit. The first time Jesus sent them out, He "gave them power over unclean spirits, to cast them out, and to heal all kinds of sickness and all kinds of disease" (Matt. 10:1). He later told an expanded group of disciples: "Behold, I give you the authority to trample on serpents and scorpions, and over all the power of the enemy" (Luke 10:19). By using that power, they were to declare the kingdom of God. They were to, "Go...and make disciples of all the nations, baptizing them in the name of the Father and of the Son and of the Holy Spirit, teaching them to observe all things that I have commanded you" (Matt. 28:19,20).

This brings us to the book of Acts, for there, more than any-where else in the Bible, we find exactly how Jesus' disciples went about implementing their Master's desire that the kingdom of God be extended.

Principles and Practice of Church Growth

F. F. Bruce says that the alternate Western reading of Acts 1:2 is slightly different from the one we ordinarily use. According to this text, Luke's Gospel had told of all that Jesus did and taught, "Until the day when he by the Holy Spirit commissioned the apostles whom he had chosen, and *commanded them to proclaim the gospel.*"[7] This is interesting, because it even more specifically casts the book of Acts into an evangelistic mode. An important part of what Jesus taught was that He had come to "build [His] church" (Matt. 16:18).

Building the Church of Jesus Christ, as described by Jesus and implemented by His followers in the book of Acts, involves the key elements of both missiology and power ministries. This is mirrored in Jesus' final words to the disciples, which we have cited previously: **But you shall receive power when the Holy Spirit has come upon you; and you shall be witnesses to Me in Jerusalem, and in all Judea and Samaria, and to the end of the earth** (Acts 1:8).

It is not easy for us today to fully comprehend what a radical concept this was to first-century Jews. Although Jesus' disciples had recollections of His ministering to a Samaritan woman, a Syrophoenician woman and a Roman centurion, their idea of the kingdom of God was still confined to the Jews, God's chosen people. They should have known better, but they didn't, and most of them wouldn't, at least for another 20 years or so.

I like the way Paul Pierson describes the implications of "Jerusalem, Judea, Samaria, and the end of the earth": "These words," says Pierson, "symbolized the breaking of an almost infinite number of barriers in order that men and women everywhere might hear and respond to the Good News. Just as God in Christ had broken through the barriers which separated eternity from time, divinity from humanity, holiness from sin, so His people were to break through geographical, racial, linguistic, religious, cultural and social barriers in order that people of every race and tongue might receive the Good News."[8] The missiological task was clear, and it was magnificently implemented in the book of Acts.

But it could not be implemented with human power alone. After three years of personal instruction, Jesus had told His disciples to "tarry in the city of Jerusalem until you are endued with power from on high" (Luke 24:49). Three years with Jesus Himself had only partially equipped them for what was ahead. They needed much more than that to engage in the spiritual warfare necessary to take the Kingdom by force (see Matt. 11:12).

The Gates of Hades

Jesus did not tell His disciples that their task was to build His Church without first warning them of the spiritual warfare it would entail. He said, "And the gates of Hades shall not prevail against it" (Matt. 16:18). He didn't say that the gates of Hades wouldn't do anything they could to hinder the growth of the Church, He just said they wouldn't *prevail*.

He also said He would give His disciples "the keys of the kingdom of heaven" (Matt. 16:19). These keys would help batter down the opposing gates of Hades. What were they? "Whatever you bind on earth will be bound in heaven, and whatever you loose on earth will be loosed in heaven" (Matt. 16:19). The Greek word for bind, *deo*, is the same word Jesus used when He spoke of binding the strongman in Matthew 12:29.

Binding the strongman, in this case Beelzebub, the ruler of the demons, is a description of what we call in today's language strategic-level spiritual warfare. Paul says, "We do not wrestle against flesh and blood, but against principalities, against powers, against the rulers of the darkness of this age, against spiritual hosts of wickedness in the heavenly places" (Eph. 6:12). Time after time in the book of Acts we will see strategic-level spiritual warfare in action: in western Cyprus with Bar-Jesus the sorcerer, in Philippi with the Python spirit, in Ephesus with Diana of the Ephesians and others.

Church Growth Reports

Luke peppers his historical account with reports of the growth of churches. (See the accompanying references from Acts.)

- The original nucleus was 120 (Acts 1:15).
- Three thousand more came on Pentecost (Acts 2:41).
- People were subsequently being added to the Church daily (Acts 2:47).
- Soon there were 5,000 men plus women and children (Acts 4:4).
- Multitudes were being saved (Acts 5:14).
- Addition changed to multiplication (Acts 6:1).
- Religious leaders began to be converted (Acts 6:7).
- Samaritans came to Christ (Acts 8:12).
- An Ethiopian was saved (Acts 8:38).
- Entire towns committed to Christ (Acts 9:35).
- A great number of Gentiles became Christians (Acts 11:21).
- A Roman proconsul believed (Acts 13:12).
- Large multitudes of Jews and Greeks accepted the faith (Acts 14:1).
- Churches increased in number daily (Acts 16:5).
- Prominent women followed Jesus (Acts 17:12).

- A ruler of the synagogue became a Christian with his household (Acts 18:8).
- **So the word of the Lord grew mightily and prevailed** (Acts 19:20).

Furthermore, Luke specifically mentions power ministries as a means toward the conversion of many individuals and communities in Acts. The complete list would be too long to reproduce, but let's take a few samples:

- On Pentecost, 3,000 were attracted through tongues.
- The process leading to the 5,000 began with Peter and John healing the lame man at the Temple gate.
- Believers were added when Peter's shadow healed some and demons were cast out.
- The gospel broke through to the Samaritans because of the miracles done through Philip.
- Many believed in Joppa because Peter raised Dorcas from the dead.
- The proconsul believed when Paul had a power encounter with Elymas the sorcerer.
- The Word of the Lord spread through Ephesus when demons were cast out through handkerchiefs blessed by Paul.

It must be clear that none of these signs and wonders by themselves saved anyone. They were accompanied by the persuasive preaching of the gospel of the death and resurrection of Jesus Christ, the promised Messiah and the Son of God. Paul says, "For I am not ashamed of the gospel of Christ, for it is the power of God to salvation for everyone who believes" (Rom. 1:16). People are born again because they put their faith in Jesus as Savior and Lord, not because they are healed or delivered. But healing and deliverance make many more open to consider the claims of Jesus

Christ than they would be without them, as we see clearly from the book of Acts.

The Outline of Acts

As I have mentioned, Acts 1:8 gives a sort of table of contents for the whole book: the evangelization of Jerusalem, Judea, Samaria and the uttermost parts of the earth. In rough outline form: Jerusalem and Judea are treated in chapters 1-7, Samaria in chapter 8 and the Gentiles in chapters 9-20. The final chapters, 21-28, deal with Paul's experiences as a prisoner of the Roman government.

Rather than write one bulky commentary on Acts, I have opted to divide it into three more manageable sections. The three volumes in this series are projected as follows:

Volume 1: *Spreading the Fire:* Acts 1-8.

Volume 2: Acts 9-15.

Volume 3: Acts 15-28.

Spreading the Fire deals with the meaning of Pentecost and how the power of the Holy Spirit has been playing a crucial role in the spread of the Church today, as it did many years ago. Healings and miracles are important. Persecutions become severe and Stephen is martyred. The young church must be properly organized and built up in faith and holiness. Peter is the key figure through this period. The first major cultural barrier is crossed when Philip evangelizes the Samaritans.

Volume 2 makes the transition from Peter to Paul with Peter's visit to the house of Cornelius, the first outreach to Gentiles. More persecution comes and James is martyred. Meanwhile, Saul of Tarsus is converted and becomes the apostle to the Gentiles: Paul. This section covers Paul's first term as a missionary in Gentile territory. His attempts to contextualize the gospel for the Gentiles are misunderstood by some members of the Jerusalem establishment and the Council of Jerusalem is convened. The conclusions of the council set the parameters for all future cross-cultural ministry.

Volume 3 covers the remainder of Paul's life and ministry. Many issues and principles related to power ministries and missiology are raised during his second and third missionary terms, not the least of which involve strenuous spiritual warfare in Philippi and Ephesus. Paul is eventually arrested and finishes his career in Rome.

Our Time Line

Not all scholars agree on the dates for the sequence of events in the book of Acts. Although the matter has been thoroughly researched by competent specialists, consensus has not yet been attained. I do not care to repeat the arguments for different time lines that are readily accessible in the various critical commentaries, but it is necessary to form an opinion. Here are some of the chief dates and events I am adopting (all dates are A.D.):

30	Pentecost
31	Persecution from fellow Jews becomes severe
32	The gospel moves from the Hebrews to the Jewish Hellenists
	Philip evangelizes Samaria
	The gospel enters North Africa
33	Saul is converted, travels to Jerusalem
34-36	Paul in Damascus, Arabia, Jerusalem
	Peter evangelizes Judea
37-45	Paul in Cilicia and Syria
	Peter continues in Judea
	The missionaries from Cyprus and Cyrene begin to win Gentiles in Antioch
46	Paul goes to Antioch
	James takes leadership of the Jerusalem church

47-48   Paul's first missionary term
49   Paul's furlough
        The Jerusalem Council
50-52   Paul's second term
52-53   Paul's second furlough
53-57   Paul's third term
57   Paul's furlough and arrest
58-61   Paul in Rome where he eventually dies
61-62   Paul's possible release (acquittal)
63-64   Paul's final arrest

Reflection Questions

1. From what you have seen in this chapter, try to tell in your own words what "missiology" and "missiologist" mean. Name some individuals known to you who might see themselves as missiologists.
2. Read Acts 1:8. Do you agree that its two major themes are power ministries and cross-cultural missions? Are you familiar with other commentaries on Acts that stress these things?
3. How important do you think Acts is as compared to the Gospels? As compared to the Epistles?
4. Do you agree that Jesus invaded Satan's kingdom? If so, name some of the ways this can affect our families or our churches or our communities.
5. Talk about the "gates of Hades." How do they enter into the picture of evangelism and church growth in Acts and today?

Notes

1. Simon J. Kistemaker, *New Testament Commentary: Exposition on the Acts of the Apostles* (Grand Rapids, MI: Baker Book House Company, 1990), p. 53. Used by permission.
2. Cf. Stanley M. Horton, *The Book of Acts* (Springfield, MO: Gospel Publishing House, 1981), pp. 21-22.
3. Cf. Paul E. Pierson, *Themes from Acts* (Ventura, CA: Regal Books, 1982), pp. 10-14. Used by permission.
4. F. F. Bruce, *The Book of Acts* (Grand Rapids, MI: William B. Eerdmans Publishing Co., 1988), p. 30. Used by permission.
5. D. Edmund Hiebert, *Personalities Around Paul* (Chicago, IL: Moody Press, 1973), p. 67.
6. Ibid., p. 74.
7. Bruce, *The Book of Acts*, p. 30.
8. Pierson, *Themes from Acts*, p. 11.

CHAPTER
2

How Jesus Attracted One Hundred Twenty Followers

The book of Acts opens with Jesus instructing His 11 apostles. They were all Jews. Later 120 people gathered in the Upper Room. They were all Jews.

Except for an isolated exception here and there, such as the Samaritan woman at the well and her friends, virtually every one of the early believers was a Jew. No intentional effort to evangelize non-Jews is recorded in the Gospels or in Acts until we come to chapter 8. There, Philip began to evangelize the half-breed Samaritans. In Acts 10, Peter visits the home of the Gentile Cornelius, but a systematic mission to plant churches among Gentiles is not recorded until Acts 11:20 where, 15 years after Pentecost, missionaries from Cyprus and Cyrene traveled to Antioch. The apostle Paul later went out from Antioch to plant churches among Gentiles, but his radical ministry became so controversial among the Jews that a summit meeting, the

Council of Jerusalem, had to be convened to help resolve the arising tensions.

The apostle Paul said that the gospel was "for the Jew first and also for the Greek" (Rom. 1:16). Why was this? Why is it that Jesus would say, "I was not sent except to the lost sheep of the house of Israel" (Matt. 15:24)? It will not be possible to adequately comprehend the radical nature of the cross-cultural missiology unfolding in the book of Acts without first going back to the Gospels and understanding how, and why, Jesus built a nucleus of 120 Jews to initiate what has now become 20 centuries of transcultural world missions.

A Theological Yes

Paul had some understandable theological reasons in saying that the gospel is for the Jews first. He had personal reasons as well. Paul was a Jew, a Hebrew of the Hebrews, who dearly loved his own people. He had such a burden for them that he once declared he would give up his own salvation if by doing so the Jewish people would follow Jesus as their Messiah (see Rom. 9:1-5).

The covenant God made with Abraham 4,000 years ago was a clear expression of God's heart for the world. He chose Abraham to be the progenitor of His special people, Israel. God's intention was to not only bless Israel, but much more. He said to Abraham, "In you *all the families of the earth* shall be blessed" (Gen. 12:3). If the Jewish people had been faithful to God's commission in the Old Testament times, history would have been different. Many Jews, even today, do not understand why history changed so radically for them when Jesus Christ came.

Paul, who became a Jewish apostle to the Gentiles, struggled much of his life, attempting to comprehend why history changed and the focus of God's activity shifted from the Jews to the Gentiles. It took him almost 25 years after his conversion to articulate it in detail, which he does in his letter to the Romans. There he says that God, true to His covenant with Abraham, brought the Messiah into the world through Jews and to the Jewish community. But Judaism, as an institution, would not accept the Messiah. They were like an olive tree whose natural branches had to be broken off and wild branches grafted in. Why? "Because of unbelief they were broken of" (Rom. 11:20). The root remained a Jewish root, but the subsequent branches of the olive tree for two millennia have been largely Gentiles. And, Paul adds, this hardening on the part of Israel will continue "until the fullness of the Gentiles has come in" (Rom. 11:25).

That is the theological yes, a clear reason to expect that the first believers in Jesus the Messiah would be Jews.

A Theological No

But there is also a theological no, a side of theology that would raise questions about such a thing.

Part of the nature of God is that He is "not willing that any should perish but that all should come to repentance" (2 Pet. 3:9). For God, "There is neither Jew nor Greek, there is neither slave nor free, there is neither male nor female" (Gal. 3:28). The clear intentions of Jesus Himself were that the gospel should spread among Gentiles as well as Jews. When He was about to depart, the Great Commission He left with His disciples was, "Go therefore and make disciples of all the nations" (Matt. 28:19). The word Jesus used for nations was *ethne*, which today we call peoples or people groups.

Jesus, of course, knew this. He was very much aware that He was the Son of God, the long awaited Messiah. He knew that when He died on the cross, the blood He shed was to be for remission of sins of whomsoever believes, Gentiles as well as Jews. Jesus knew He was beginning a process of redemption that would end with a great multitude in heaven composed of "all nations, tribes, peoples, and tongues standing before the throne and before the Lamb" (Rev. 7:9).

So the question persists: Why were the 120 who surrounded Jesus all Jews? Why didn't Jesus follow the pattern of one modern pastor who said he was praying for "a heterogeneous church, a group of believers that was a microcosm of the church universal. If persons from all walks of life, cultures, races, church affiliations, and doctrinal divergencies make up the true Body of Christ...why could we not in one local church have the same diversity?" Why, during the three years of His public ministry, did Jesus not win some Jews first to honor the Abrahamic covenant, but also include some Ethiopians or Lystrans or Samaritans or Macedonians or Venelli or Vercingetorix or Atuatuci, just to name a few of the diverse people groups of that time and place?

Presumably, Jesus' reasons for maintaining Jewish homogeneity, rather than attempting multicultural heterogeneity, could not have been entirely theological. Theologically, He had come to announce the kingdom of God not only for Jews, but also for all of the above people groups and many more as well. Having a mixture in His own nucleus that represented the diversity of the ethnic multitude around the throne in heaven would seem to be more politically correct and theologically correct than having a nucleus of all Jews.

If the underlying reasons were not exclusively *theological*, it could well be they were also *methodological*. Under the assumption that Jesus had planned a systematic strategy for His three short years of ministry as opposed to happenstance, could it be that He intended to set a pattern for the future of Christian missions? If so, Jesus might have been modeling a principle that plays a key role in contemporary missiology called "the people approach to world evangelization."

The People Approach to World Evangelization

The people approach to world evangelization is based on a high view of culture. As Donald McGavran says, "People like to become Christians without crossing racial, linguistic, or class barriers."[1] Culture is something most people do not take lightly, as anthropologists are quick to inform us. Violating or denigrating the way of life or the way of thinking of a people group has proven to be a poor way of subsequently attracting them to the gospel of Christ, even though the gospel has clearly transcultural dimensions.

Although there may be some variations and exceptions, modern missiology teaches that the most viable strategy for extending the kingdom of God throughout the world is to set targets, people group by people group. What is a people group? Today's chief missiological catalytic organizations, the A.D. 2000 and Beyond Movement and its predecessor, the Lausanne Committee for World Evangelization, have agreed on this definition:

> A people group is a significantly large sociological grouping of individuals who perceive themselves to have a common affinity for one another. From the viewpoint of evangelization this is the largest possible group within which the gospel can spread without encountering barriers of understanding or acceptance.

Apparently, Jesus considered the Jews as one such people group. Among them, a considerable variety ranged from Matthew, who was a tax collector for the Roman government, to Simon, who was a Zealot bent on overthrowing the Roman government. But beyond differences in political positions, age and disposition, they belonged to the same ethnic group, had the same color skin, shared similar cultural values, including prejudices, ate and abstained from the same foods, spoke the same language and perceived themselves to have a common affinity for one another.

Jesus knew well that the people approach is the best approach to evangelization. As McGavran says, "It may be taken as axiomatic that whenever becoming a Christian is a racial rather than a religious decision, there the growth of the church will be exceedingly slow."[2] He then adds, "The great obstacles to conversion are social, not theological."[3] I realize that what I have just said is, to many, a controversial issue. But I can assure them that it is sound missiology.

How Important Is Culture?

If the people approach to world evangelization is based on a high view of culture, how can this be justified? Culture is frequently seen as something that provokes separation and social disharmony. Some think of culture as an evil that needs to be ignored, if not stamped out. A goal is to assimilate all peoples into one language and culture.

In today's world, however, such a goal is seen as unrealistic idealism. A new respect for culture is developing. The United States now thinks of itself as a multicultural society rather than a melting pot. This is a more biblical way of thinking, because God Himself is the creator of human cultures. Three important biblical insights help us understand multiculturalism in a positive light:

The human race is one. All the diverse peoples of the earth ultimately belong to one family. God created Adam and Eve to be the progenitors of all of humankind. Traced back far enough, every human is genetically related to every other. The apostle Paul affirms this in his sermon on Mars Hill in Athens: **He [God] has made from one blood every nation of men to dwell on all the face of the earth, and has determined their preappointed times and the boundaries of their habitation (Acts 17:26).**

This is the basis for the biblical affirmation that in the community of the Kingdom there is no difference between Jews and Gentiles.

God intended humans to be diverse. Although it is true that the kingdom of God admits Jews and Gentiles on an equal basis, it is equally true that in this present life they are distinct. As I interpret the biblical evidence, I see this distinction and the uniqueness of all people groups as part of God's creative design. Biologically speaking, the genes and chromosomes of Adam and Eve must have contained all the genetic material for the human diversity we see today.

The first biblical list of human people groups occurs in Genesis 10, called by some "The Table of the Nations." Each people was "separated into their lands, everyone according to his own language, according to their families, into their nations" (Gen. 10:5). The way this came about is narrated in Genesis 11, through the well-known story of the Tower of Babel, where, in one fell swoop, God decided to "confuse their language, that they may not understand one another's speech" (Gen. 11:7).

Biblical scholars have at least two opinions about God's underlying motivation for confusing the languages. One of them is expressed by Gerhard von Rad, who sees the outcome of Babel as "disorder in the international world...[that] was not willed by God but is punishment for the sinful rebellion against God."[4] This is a very common interpretation, which surfaces frequently in sermons on racial reconciliation.

Von Rad's negative interpretation, however, is not compatible either with a Christian understanding of cultural anthropology or with contemporary views of missiological strategy. Suggesting that cultural diversity is rooted in human sin rather than in the purpose of God's creation is clearly not the only way to understand Genesis 10 and 11. I, for one, see it differently.

The other point of view regards the sinful rebellion of the human race at the Tower of Babel as an effort to *prevent* the human race from becoming diversified according to God's plan. From the beginning, God had set in motion His design to separate humans into people groups so that they could best, "Be fruitful and multiply; fill the earth," as He said to Adam (Gen. 1:28). However, the early human race, which still all spoke one language (see Gen. 11:1), rebelled against this plan. They intuitively perceived that as they multiplied, families and clusters of families would need more land for farming and hunting and that if they continued to scatter, their social separation would eventually produce increasing cultural differentiation.

Knowing there was no human way to prevent this, they sought supernatural power to assist them. They could not turn to God, for the scattering was His own plan. Instead, they turned to the satanic powers of darkness to implement their plans for a one-world movement. They built the Tower of Babel, which archaeologists identify as a typical ancient ziggurat, an overtly occultic structure. They wanted the tower to have its "top...in the heavens" (Gen. 11:4) in order to commune directly with the demonic principalities they had agreed to serve. And the reason they started building the tower and the city around it was clearly stated: "Lest we be scattered abroad over the face of the whole earth" (Gen. 11:4). Their supreme fear was to allow God to diversify them, and they were willing to make a pact with the devil in order to prevent it.

Their scheme did not work, as we well know. God sovereignly intervened and accomplished in an instant what He might have ordinarily taken centuries or millennia to do—He changed the monolingual society to a multilingual society. This effectively stopped the building of the tower and the city, and rapidly accelerated the geographical scattering of the people groups, each now with its own language.

Bernhard Anderson, Professor of Old Testament theology at Princeton Seminary, agrees that God's original will for the human race was dispersion and diversity. He says, "When the Babel story is read in its literary context there is no basis for the negative view that pluralism is God's judgment upon human sinfulness. Diversity is not a condemnation....God's will for His creation is diversity rather than homogeneity. Ethnic pluralism is to be welcomed as a divine blessing."[5]

In my opinion, this high view of human culture and its origins is a valuable building block for formulating a sound biblical and practical missiology.

God is concerned to bring all peoples to Himself. Paul speaks of Jesus Christ as the "only Potentate, the King of kings and Lord of lords" (1 Tim. 6:15). As we have said many times, God sent His Son to die so that "this gospel of the kingdom will be preached in all the world as a witness to all the nations" (Matt. 24:14).

The way God's master plan has been, and is being, implemented most effectively in the world today is through the people approach to world evangelization.

Not All Evangelism Is the Same

In order to sort out the most appropriate evangelistic methodologies for spreading the gospel to all the peoples of the world, some helpful terminology has been developed, using the symbols E-1, E-2 and E-3. The "E" stands for evangelism and the numbers stand for the barriers that must be crossed in order to do it.

E-1 evangelism. E-1 is monocultural evangelism. The only barrier is to move outside the Church, which presumably is a community of believers, into the world, where the unbelievers are found. For many, this "stained glass barrier" is a formidable one, and all too many Christians fail to cross it. They do not have to learn a new language; they do not have to eat different food; they do not have to adapt to new behavior patterns. Their job is to communicate the good news to people very much like themselves.

E-2 and E-3 evangelism. Both of these are cross-cultural, and the difference between the two is one of degree. E-2 implies crossing the same "stained glass barrier" as E-1, but also one degree of cultural barrier. E-3 involves a more distant cultural barrier. For instance, Anglo-Americans evangelizing Mexican-Americans would be E-2 because the two cultures have comparatively minor differences. The same Anglo-Americans evangelizing Masai in Kenya would find themselves in an E-3 situation because the culture there is radically different.

Keep in mind that the distinction here is cultural, not geographic. In multicultural urban societies in America, for example, opportunities for E-1, E-2 and E-3 can at times be found in the same neighborhood or even the same city block.

Obviously, most people, year in and year out, are won to Christ through E-1 evangelism. Most evangelists are monocultural evangelists. Most pastors are monocultural pastors. It has always been this way and it always will be. The reason for this is very simple. God has called and equipped most people to minister primarily to those of their own culture. But not all.

God has also called some to minister with whatever spiritual gifts they have in different cultures. If He hadn't, Christianity would never have become a universal religion. Those whom God has called to minister in E-2 and E-3 situations, He also equips with the missionary gift. In my book *Your Spiritual Gifts Can Help Your Church Grow*, I define the missionary gift as follows:

> The gift of missionary is the special ability that God gives to certain members of the Body of Christ to minister whatever other spiritual gifts they have in a second culture.[6]

Given the fact that somewhere between 6,000 and 12,000 unreached people groups are yet to be reached with the gospel, it may come as a surprise to learn, as I indicate in my book *Your Spiritual Gifts Can Help Your Church Grow*, that less than one percent of committed Christians have been given the missionary gift. Low as this might sound, considerably fewer than half this number of Christians around the world are actively engaged in cross-cultural ministries. If as many as one percent were ever mobilized and trained, the resulting missionary force would be more than adequate to reach all of the unreached in our present generation.

How can it be done with so few?

It goes back to the fact that most evangelism is monocultural. The job for cross-cultural missionaries is to implant the gospel in a new people group by E-2 or E-3 ministry, then to equip the nationals there to continue the task by using E-1. We frequently hear the expression, "Nationals can evangelize better than missionaries." This is true because E-1 is the easiest, most natural and most effective kind of evangelism.

Jesus Was Monocultural

This brings us back to the main issue of this chapter. Why is it that Jesus' nucleus of 120 were all Jews? It is because Jesus, representing 99 percent of Christian people, was monocultural. In Jesus' human ministry, the Father had called and equipped Him as an E-1 evangelist. I say His *human* ministry because as the eternal Son of God, Jesus crossed an awesome barrier by taking on a human nature and becoming a servant, as we read in Philippians 2:5-8. This was unique, however; something none of us could ever identify with. Most of us, on the other hand, can easily identify with Jesus' E-1 monocultural human ministry.

As I said before, I believe that Jesus' three years of monocultural ministry to the Jews was more of a strategic than a theological choice. As far as we know from the Scriptures, Jesus did not train any of His 12 disciples for cross-cultural ministry, although subsequent tradition indicates that some of them may have become missionaries. The possibility that Thomas went to India or that Matthew went to Ethiopia would be examples. Nevertheless, the first E-3 missionary appearing in Acts would be Philip when he preached to the Samaritans (see Acts 8:5). More radical E-3 missionaries would be those who went from Cyprus and Cyrene to the Gentiles in Antioch (see Acts 11:20), and the most outstanding one would be Paul, known as the apostle to the Gentiles. But none of the above was a member of Jesus' nucleus of 120.

Now, let's examine as closely as we can just how Jesus went about His ministry, because 99 percent of us will be using similar methods and strategy.

The World as Jesus Found It

The geopolitical world into which Jesus was born and in which He went about His ministry was the Roman Empire. By that time, the central government in Rome had gained political control of about 30 provinces, each with its own ethnic and cultural mixes. The Christian faith began as an insignificant Jewish sect on the eastern end of the Mediterranean Sea. In only 70 years, it had become a prominent feature on the religious landscape of the Roman Empire, and three centuries later it was declared the Empire's official religion!

Looking at the ethnology of the Roman Empire from the perspective of Jesus and the apostles, the major division was between Jews and Gentiles. It has been estimated that Jews comprised around 8 percent of the population of the Roman Empire of 90 million people. That would calculate to slightly more than 7 million Jews.

Social relationships between Jews and Gentiles were exceedingly strained. A. C. Bouquet comments, "We have perhaps no parallel to it in the world today other than that in India between strict Brahmins and non-Brahmins, and it was more severe in some ways even than this."[7] Jews alienated Gentiles when the Jews refused to:

- Eat anything but certified kosher food;
- Go near a Gentile temple;
- Enter a Gentile home;
- Drink milk drawn from a cow by a Gentile;
- Use Gentile drinking cups;
- Leave a Gentile alone in a Jewish home;
- Sell cattle to a Gentile.

Gentiles reacted to such behavior with scorn, ridicule and reverse discrimination. Anti-Semitism was pervasive. Jews were regarded as a despised minority by most Gentiles. It is not difficult, therefore, to understand why Jewish believers felt that unclean Gentiles should not be admitted to the Church unless they first agreed to become Jewish proselytes through circumcision and vowed to obey the Jewish law.

The Gentiles, of course, were not all the same. Many people groups, having a great diversity of languages, ethnicity and cultures, were included within the general category of Roman Gentiles.

Jews were not all the same either. Hebrews and Hellenists were quite distinct. Among the Hebrews themselves, Judeans and Galileans had differing cultures. A variety of subgroups of Hellenistic Jews were molded to one degree or another by the particular city or province in which they lived. There were several religious groups such as Pharisees and Sadducees, plus predictable socioeconomic divisions.

Between the Jews and Gentiles, were the mixed-blood

Samaritans, a community of Jews who had long before intermar-
ried with Gentiles. Jews avoided Samaritans as adamantly as they
did Gentiles (see John 4:9).

The world into which God sent His Son, then, was a highly
diversified cultural mosaic. It was a formidable evangelistic and
missiological challenge.

Jesus Gathers His Inner Circle

After He was baptized by John the Baptist, Jesus began His three
years of public ministry. One of the priority items on His agenda
was to recruit a ministry team. He naturally began calling His disciples among fellow Jews who had been waiting for generations
for the promised Messiah. One of the more devout was Andrew,
a disciple of John the Baptist, who was present at Jesus' baptism
in the Jordan River. After Andrew met Jesus, he immediately
went to his brother, Simon Peter, and said, "We have found the
Messiah" (John 1:41).

Soon Philip and Nathanael were added. Nathanael was another Jew who was so receptive that he exclaimed, "Rabbi, You are
the Son of God! You are the King of Israel!" (John 1:49). Then
Simon Peter's fishing partners, James and John, decided to leave
their fishing business to join Jesus' inner circle.

This is the way E-1 evangelism ordinarily happens. For one
thing, all being Jews, they did not consider their decision to follow Jesus a racial issue. This fits with Donald McGavran's statement, cited earlier, that whenever becoming a Christian is seen
as a racial decision rather than a personal commitment to Jesus or
a religious decision, little church growth can be expected.
Nothing in the apostles' decision involved a betrayal of their
non-Christian kith and kin. By following Jesus, they were not
becoming less Jewish than before.

The door was then open for outreach along natural lines.

Andrew moved along family lines and found his brother Peter. Peter moved along vocational lines and found fellow fishermen, James and John. Andrew and Peter moved along community lines and found Philip, who lived in their hometown of Bethsaida and who, in all probability, grew up together with them as children. In all, the issue was not how Jewish they would continue to be, but whether or not they would recognize Jesus as the Messiah, the Son of God and the King of Israel.

When the apostle Paul says that the gospel is "for the Jew first" (Rom. 1:16), it fits perfectly into the pattern established by Jesus. He could have done it in no other way and seen the same positive results. If, instead of doing this, Jesus had gone back to Egypt where He lived as a baby and attempted to draw together an inner circle of Gentile Egyptians, it is not unreasonable to suspect that little or nothing would have happened.

None of this is to detract in any way from the deity of Jesus Christ or the sovereignty of God. It is simply based on the assumption that Jesus' intent was to model a way of doing evangelism that could be applied for generations to come by human individuals who would not have a divine nature such as He had.

What Kind of Jews?

I am familiar with the viewpoint of some idealists that Jesus' inner circle of 12 was characterized by great diversity. This would be true only as far as diversity of age, occupation, formal education, social class, personality types and political preferences might be concerned. It would not be true of race or ethnicity. Obviously, there were no Gentiles or Samaritans of any kind. But, less obviously, none of the Jews was a *Hellenistic Jew* of the dispersion who might have been raised in Tarsus or Antioch or Pontus. Every one was a *Hebrew Jew* raised in Palestine. Although they were all Jews, important differences between

Hebrews and Hellenists carried over into the Church, as we will clearly see when we come to Acts 6. Then we read, **There arose a murmuring against the Hebrews by the Hellenists** (Acts 6:1), showing that even conversion to Christ would not totally erase such subcultural differences.

Was Jesus a Hillbilly?
But that is not all. No Hebrew Jew of first-century Palestine would have been unaware of the differences between those from Judea to the south as opposed to those from Galilee to the north. Jesus, although born in Bethlehem of Judea and resident for a time in Egypt, was known as a native of Nazareth in Galilee. A common designation for Him was "Jesus of Nazareth." What difference would this make?

I hope I am not interpreted as being irreverent when I report that in those days Galilee was seen much as some Americans see Appalachia in our day. Galileans were commonly regarded by Judeans as hillbillies. If they fit the patterns we are accustomed to, they had their own musical taste, their distinctive foods, their way of life and they spoke Aramaic with a hillbilly accent. They were called *Am ha-aretz*, "people of the land."

Jesus was one of them, and would have been regarded as culturally disadvantaged by many sophisticated Jerusalemites. Significantly, Jesus selected those for His inner circle, with one exception, from fellow Galileans. A clear indication that they kept their hillbilly accent occurred when Peter later attempted to deny that he was one of the inner circle, but the people of Jerusalem could not be fooled. They said, "Surely you also are one of them, because your speech betrays you" (Matt. 26:73). Later, those of the Jerusalem Sanhedrin characterized Peter and John as **uneducated and untrained men** (Acts 4:13), not a complimentary remark. None of Jesus' inner circle was a Pharisee, a priest, a scholar or an Essene, although all of them would also have been Hebrew Jews.

The one possible non-Galilean might have been Judas Iscariot. John Broadus points out that Iscariot could signify *Ish Kerioth*, Aramaic for "a man of Kerioth." Kerioth was a village in Judea, so Judas may well have been a Judean.[8] It scarcely needs to be mentioned that Judas was the most obvious misfit of the 12. He became a traitor and left the group.

Who replaced Judas? The two candidates were Matthias, who was another Galilean, and Joseph Barsabas, who was likely a Hellenistic Jew from Cyprus. Matthias, as we know, was selected by casting lots, a method, at that time, apparently regarded as allowing the Holy Spirit to express His will. So the reorganized 12 represented a relatively small slice of the demographic mix of the day.

Jesus Ministered to Jews

According to E. A. Judge, Jesus' ministry team largely worked with other Aramaic-speaking Jews from the provincial "backwater" of Galilee. Judge says that the area of Galilee was geographically limited and "emotionally the gulf between it and the civilized world was profound. The real division was of course cultural."[9]

When Jesus traveled outside Galilee to Decapolis, a group of republics, He was declared *persona non grata* even though He had cast a demon out of a man who had been terrorizing the people there. Then an interesting thing happened. The former demoniac was so grateful to Jesus for delivering him that he volunteered his services to his new Master (see Mark 5:18). Some would have expected that Jesus would gladly have received him in order to demonstrate the multicultural nature of the Body of Christ. But Jesus did not allow him to join His band of Galileans and go with them back to Galilee. Rather, He instructed him, "Go home to your friends, and tell them what great things the Lord has done for you" (Mark 5:19). Jesus apparently thought the Gadarene would be more effective doing E-1 evangelism than the E-2 for which he had volunteered.

One of Jesus' more specific statements about the planned scope of His ministry arose in His dialogue with a Greek Syrophoenician woman who wanted her daughter healed. Jesus graciously healed her daughter, but not until He had made it clear that this would be an exception to His pattern of ministering to Jews. He said, "I was not sent except to the lost sheep of the house of Israel" (Matt. 15:24).

The Gospel of John tells of some Gentiles who had come to Jerusalem to worship Jehovah God and who requested an interview with Jesus. Philip and Andrew related the request to Jesus, but nothing is subsequently said of Jesus ever granting the interview (see John 12:20-22).

It seems that when Jesus had occasion to go to Judea, He frequently stayed in Bethany with His friends Lazarus, Mary and Martha. However, the probability is that they were fellow Galileans who lived in Judea, but also maintained a residence in Galilee. For example, some think the well-known incident when Jesus commended Mary for sitting at His feet occurred in their home in Galilee (see Luke 10:38), not in Judea.

When Jesus first sent out His 12 disciples on their own, He was very specific about the people group they were to seek out for ministry. He said, "Do not go into the way of the Gentiles, and do not enter a city of the Samaritans" (Matt. 10:5). Rather, He instructed them to stick to their own people group, "the lost sheep of the house of Israel" (Matt. 10:6).

Jesus So Loved the World

None of what has been said should be interpreted to mean that Jesus, the Son of man, was ethnocentric, prejudiced or indifferent to the salvation of non-Jews. He was God and He loved the whole world. But He was also building a solid nucleus for a movement that would be carried on through centuries to come by human beings, and He was modeling evangelistic strategy for them. He knew that if Christianity were to spread to the whole world, it first must have a firm foundation, and that such a foundation could best be established among Aramaic-speaking Galilean Jews.

Jesus did cross boundaries. In preparation for His Great Commission to "make disciples of all the nations" (Matt. 28:19), Jesus ministered to a Roman centurion's servant and commended the centurion for his faith, a faith even greater than He had found in Israel (see Matt. 8:5-13). Jesus spent two days in Samaria and demonstrated to His disciples that salvation would also be available for those such as the Samaritan woman and her friends (see John 4:5-43). After the healed demoniac had prepared the way, Jesus went back to Decapolis and fed 4,000 (see Matt. 15:32-39). In a parable, Jesus commended a good Samaritan (see Luke 10:30-37) for crossing a cultural barrier.

These incidents were living demonstrations of the universality of the gospel, but they were relatively minor episodes on the whole time line of Jesus' earthly ministry. After each, He soon continued His ministry to "the lost sheep of the house of Israel" (Matt. 15:24).

Back to Jerusalem

Jesus ended His ministry, not in Galilee, but in Jerusalem. This brings us into the book of Acts, where we will continue from here on.

It may be that among the 120 who gathered in the Upper Room, several were by then non-Galileans. Barsabas, as we have said, was possibly a Cyprian (see Acts 1:23), and others may also have been non-Galileans. Nevertheless, they were mostly

Galileans. After Jesus' ascension, two angels appeared and addressed those who had witnessed it as, **Men of Galilee** (Acts 1:11). And then, on the Day of Pentecost, part of the amazement of the unbelievers when they heard the gospel being proclaimed in a variety of languages was, **Are not all these who speak Galileans?** (Acts 2:7).

In summary: The reason the 120 in the Upper Room were all Jews was not only that the gospel was to come to "the Jew first." Jesus could have done that by winning 60 Jews and adding another 60 of a multicultural mix of Gentiles and Samaritans. But, instead, He showed us that in order to accomplish His ultimate purpose of making disciples of all nations, a solid foundation needed to be built by using E-1 evangelism within a given people group.

The book of Acts, subsequently, shows how such a committed nucleus can move out in the power of God to break down every possible remaining barrier to world evangelization.

Reflection Questions

1. Discuss the reasons Jesus did not include any non-Jews such as Gentiles or Samaritans in His inner circle or in the 120 disciples He left behind in Jerusalem.
2. Why would the "people approach to world evangelism" be seen by missiologists as the most viable way to plan strategies for world evangelization?
3. Do you agree that God's original design was that the human race would be diversified into many cultural groups and that the incident at the Tower of Babel mainly served to accelerate this process?

4. Discuss the differences between Hebrew Jews and Hellenistic Jews. Then discuss the difference between Judean Hebrews and Galilean Hebrews. Where does Jesus fit into this picture?
5. Give some biblical illustrations to show that Jesus desired that the gospel eventually would be spread among the world's non-Jews.

Notes

1. Donald A. McGavran, *Understanding Church Growth* (Grand Rapids, MI: William B. Eerdmans Publishing Co., Third Edition, 1990), p. 163. Used by permission.
2. Ibid., p. 155.
3. Ibid., p. 156.
4. Gerhard von Rad, *Genesis: A Commentary*, tr. John H. Marks (Louisville, KY: Westminster Press, 1961), p. 148.
5. Bernhard Anderson, "The Babel Story: Paradigm of Human Unity and Diversity," *Ethnicity*, edited by Andrew M. Greeley and Gregory Baum (New York: The Seabury Press, 1977), p. 68.
6. C. Peter Wagner, *Your Spiritual Gifts Can Help Your Church Grow* (Ventura, CA: Regal Books, 1994), p. 179.
7. A. C. Bouquet, *Everyday Life in New Testament Times* (New York: Charles Scribner's Sons, 1953), p. 16.
8. John A. Broadus, *Commentary on the Gospel of Matthew* (Philadelphia, PA: American Baptist Publishing Society, 1886), p. 211.
9. E. A. Judge, *The Social Pattern of the Christian Groups in the First Century* (London, England: Tyndale, 1960), p. 15.

CHAPTER

3

Acts 1

History's Most Powerful Prayer Meeting

Acts 1
Bridging from Luke's Gospel to Acts

> 1. The former account I made, O Theophilus, of all that Jesus began both to do and teach, 2. until the day in which He was taken up, after He through the Holy Spirit had given commandments to the apostles whom He had chosen.

I have already explained how we know that Luke is the author of Acts, which, along with Luke's Gospel, comprises a two-volume account of the origins and expansions of the Christian movement. In summarizing his Gospel, Luke mentions that it covers the things Jesus began **both to do and teach**. Here, two things are particularly significant.

Doing and Teaching Go Together

When Jesus walked with the two disciples on the road to Emmaus after His resurrection, He asked them what they were talking about. They responded, "The things concerning Jesus of Nazareth, who was a Prophet mighty *in deed and word* before God and all the people" (Luke 24:19). Some are attracted by philosophers whose ideas are so fascinating that applying their ideas to their practical, everyday life is not particularly significant. Others are attracted by flamboyant wonder-workers or self-flagellating ascetics who are not capable of undergirding their lifestyles with sensible explanations of their behavior. Jesus was neither of the above. He preached what He practiced, and practiced what He preached.

Doing Comes Before Teaching

I do not think it is an accident that in both Acts and his Gospel, Luke puts practicing before preaching, doing before teaching, deed before word. Whereas, some theologians suggest that sound theology precedes fruitful ministry, the opposite is usually the case. It is significant that Jesus never wrote a theology, although His teachings were saturated with theologically significant truths that theologians continue to analyze almost 2,000 years later. Of all the New Testament books, the one that comes closest to a theology is the Epistle to the Romans, which Paul wrote 30 years after gospel preaching began.

The Protestant Reformation was implemented in practice before Luther and Calvin, to say nothing of Kuyper and Barth and Henry, attempted to systematize its theology. When William Carey decided to go to India as a missionary, he received no encouragement from the recognized theologians of the day. Subsequently, however, excellent, theologically informed missiology has emerged from the modern missionary movement Carey initiated by moving out in ministry.

Even in the world of rapid change in which we now live, it is not unusual for theology to find itself about 10 years behind practice. For example, I was deeply involved with John Wimber through the early and mid-eighties, introducing the signs and wonders movement into mainstream evangelicalism. I could not have written my book *How To Have a Healing Ministry in Any Church* until I had personally participated in healing ministries for several years. Furthermore, few will consider my book a *theology* of signs and wonders. Some important, theologically informed books by authors such as Ken Blue[1] and Don Williams[2] were written in the early years. But the more mature theological works, such as Jack Deere's *Surprised by the Power of the Spirit* (Zondervan) and Gary Greig and Kevin Springer's *The Kingdom and the Power* (Regal Books), were not published until 1993, more than 10 years after the ministry itself began to spread.

One of the few credentialed theologians who frankly recognizes that deed comes before word is Ray Anderson of Fuller Theological Seminary. His thesis is that "ministry precedes and produces theology, not the reverse." Anderson says that Jesus' "ministry was to do the will of the Father and...out of this ministry emerges theological activity."[3]

By this, I do not mean to imply that the theology is incidental or unnecessary. Far from it. Now that sound theologies of signs and wonders and other power ministries are emerging, ministries characterized by supernatural manifestations of the power of the Holy Spirit will spread throughout the Body of Christ even more rapidly and with more integrity than they have previously. My point is that in this case, as in the life of Jesus, deed usually preceded word.

Jesus Used Holy Spirit Power

2. ...after He through the Holy Spirit...

How could it be that Jesus would have said to His disciples, "He who believes in Me, the works that I do he will do also; and greater works than these will he do, because I go to My Father" (John 14:12)? The reason certainly cannot be that Jesus will make those of us who follow Him into gods with divine natures such as Jesus had. A much more plausible reason would be that we, as human beings, will have access to the same source of supernatural power that Jesus had, namely, the Holy Spirit.

It is very helpful to understand this before we come to the words of Jesus later in this chapter, **But you shall receive power when the Holy Spirit has come upon you** (Acts 1:8). As we move through Acts, we will see that such was actually the case: Jesus' followers duplicated the power ministries He demonstrated and even did some things Jesus Himself did not do.

As the second Person of the Trinity, Jesus was the only individual who ever existed as 100 percent God and 100 percent human. The doctrine of the two natures of Christ is one of biblical Christianity's theological nonnegotiables. Although Jesus was never without all the attributes of God, He, nevertheless, voluntarily gave up the *use* of these attributes during His incarnation, living, ministering and even thinking with His human nature only. How, then, did He do all the supernatural works and exhibit divine knowledge? **Through the Holy Spirit**, as Luke indicates in this passage.

This is why Fuller Seminary theologian Colin Brown has coined the term "Spirit Christology." He says, "Jesus' miracles are given a prominent place, but they are not attributed to Jesus as the Second Person of the Trinity. They are not presented as manifestations of His personal divinity."[4] Thomas A. Smail is also very specific: "If His miracles had nothing to do with His humanity, if divine power was not communicated to His human nature as a charismatic gift, then obviously that power has nothing to do with our humanity either."[5] But a key to understanding the book of Acts, and using it as a training manual for ministry today, is recognizing that the power of the Holy Spirit that operated in Jesus also operated in the apostles and can operate in us as well.

I am fully aware that theologians continue to debate this point, and that here I am giving it an extremely short treatment. Those who wish to know my opinion on this can find a more complete argument in my book *How to Have a Healing Ministry in Any Church*. But to make one more point, consider Peter's words later in Acts: **God anointed Jesus of Nazareth with the Holy Spirit and with power, who went about doing good and healing all who were oppressed by the devil, for God was with Him** (Acts 10:38). Because God is the source of all power, there is no way He, as God, could be anointed, ever. God needs absolutely nothing outside of Himself to do anything at all. It is clear, then, that the reference to Jesus' receiving the anointing of the Holy Spirit and power cannot possibly refer to His divine nature, and, therefore, must have been performed only on His human nature. It was Jesus' human nature, **through the Holy Spirit**, as our text affirms.

Things Pertaining to the Kingdom

3. to whom He also presented Himself alive after His suffering by many infallible proofs, being seen by them during forty days and speaking of the things pertaining to the kingdom of God.

Between His resurrection and ascension, Jesus spent about six weeks with His disciples. His topic was the kingdom of God. As I explained in chapter 1, an understanding of the kingdom of God provides for us a solid theological framework to apply what we learn from the ministry of Jesus, and the subsequent Acts of the Apostles, to our own churches and communities today.

The most concrete, lasting form of ministry in Acts is church planting. Preaching the gospel, healing the sick, casting out demons, suffering persecution, holding church councils and the multiple other activities of the apostles and other Christians that unfold before us have, as their goal, multiplying Christian churches throughout the known world. Related to His teaching of the kingdom, I would surmise that Jesus often repeated His purpose statement, "I will build My church" (Matt. 16:18). He had reserved disclosing this to His disciples until in Caesarea Philippi they had finally understood, "You are the Christ, the Son of the living God" (Matt. 16:16). His resurrection later confirmed forever by **infallible proofs** that Jesus was the true Messiah for whom the Jews had waited for centuries.

For Jesus, the kingdom of God had come, although the kingdom should not be overly identified with the Church. Over the years, many institutional forms of the Christian Church have evolved that are far from what Jesus had in mind as He was instructing His disciples. Without naming names, it is a fact that all too much of what is known as Christianity is actively promulgating both deeds and words that are contrary to what we know of the kingdom of God, not a reflection of God's will in the world today. Such so-called "churches" are not to be identified with the kingdom of God. But, at the same time, multitudes of churches in many parts of the world, although imperfectly, do accurately reflect the glory of God through Jesus Christ and, as such, can be considered visible outposts of the kingdom of God.

Churches that adhere to biblical standards are not the only, but are still the most tangible, manifestations we have today of answers to our prayer, "Your kingdom come. Your will be done on earth as it is in heaven" (Matt. 6:10). Believers redeemed by the blood of Jesus Christ who meet together to worship and praise the triune God on a regular basis, and who minister to others doing good in Jesus' name, legitimately represent the Kingdom here in this world.

The Promise of the Father

4. And being assembled together with them, He command‑ed them not to depart from Jerusalem, but to wait for the Promise of the Father, "which," He said, "you have heard from Me."

Soon after His resurrection, Jesus told His disciples to wait in Jerusalem, as Luke records in his Gospel: "Behold, I send the Promise of My Father upon you; but tarry in the city of Jerusalem until you are endued with power from on high" (Luke 24:49). This was quite an unusual thing. Here were the disciples who had been with Jesus personally for three years. He had thoroughly instructed them through both deed and word in theology, in ethics, in worship and in ministry. He had sent them out on their own for supervised field experience. And yet, this superb training had not fully equipped them for the task Jesus had set before them. Knowing the right thing to do is not enough. Supernatural power is necessary for God's purposes to be fulfilled.

It is easy to get caught up in techniques and methodology, especially when they have produced positive results in the past, such as Jesus' ministry had. The church growth movement, of which I am a part, began to succumb to this tendency toward the end of the '70s when the movement was around 25 years old. At that time, some of our critics began to complain that we had begun to rely on human technology instead of spiritual power. The dangers of such a trap are obvious. The kingdom of God cannot successfully invade the kingdom of Satan by human ingenuity alone, but only by being endued with power from on high. Many of us listened to our critics and asked God to correct us, which He has been doing since the beginning of the 1980s.

As God began to change us, He stretched us beyond some of our comfort zones. Many of us had reacted strongly against the Pentecostal movement, for example, saying that what we considered their excesses had taken them far beyond the boundaries of respectable, biblical Christianity. Among other things, we had convinced ourselves that Pentecostals were hyperemotional and uneducated. We scarcely stopped to realize that the Pharisees entertained a similar attitude toward Jesus and the apostles, whom they regarded as uneducated Galilean hillbillies. So, like the Pharisees, we had developed protective, sophisticated theologies, including modern cessationist dispensationalism. I, along with fellow seminary professors, such as Charles Kraft and Jack Deere, had convinced myself and, therefore, many of my students that gifts manifesting supernatural power, such as healings and prophecies and tongues and deliverance, had ceased at the end of the Apostolic Age.

But God had other things in store for us, and the three of us, along with increasing numbers of traditional evangelicals, more recently have experienced "paradigm shifts" that have allowed us to begin to understand the Promise of the Father. Charles Kraft and I shifted our paradigms through seeing power ministry firsthand from John Wimber, then beginning to practice it ourselves. You can read about these experiences in our books *Christianity with Power* (Kraft, Servant Books) and *How to Have a Healing Ministry in Any Church* (Wagner, Regal Books). Jack Deere explains how he changed his point of view, by seriously restudying the Scriptures, in his book *Surprised by the Power of the Spirit* (Zondervan).

I mention these because they represent a widespread trend in the Body of Christ. Although some Christian leaders are still reluctant, the general worldwide movement is toward power ministries not toward cessationism. Power ministries, and how they should be applied, constitute a crucial theme throughout the book of Acts, as I have mentioned. Unfortunately, many of the other 1,398 commentaries on Acts assume the cessationist point of view.

My parallel theme in interpreting Acts is missiology, by which I mean the more technological and methodological sides of evangelism and church planting. By putting all the stress here on **the Promise of the Father**, I do not want to leave the impression that we are to choose between power and missiological technology. I believe the two must go together like the two wings on a bird. Neither technology nor power *by itself* will effectively fulfill Jesus' Great Commission. We will see multiple examples of this as we continue through the book of Acts.

Tarry—But Not Forever

4. ...wait for the Promise of the Father.

The disciples never could have become dynamic instruments for the extension of the kingdom of God if they had not obeyed Jesus' command to wait for the Promise of the Father or to "tarry...until you are endued with power from on high" (Luke 24:49). It is notable that the tarrying took all of 10 days, no longer.

In Christian service, there is a delicate balance between spending time with the Father in worship, praise and intimacy, and in obeying the Father's commands in ministry and outreach. The Upper Room, where the disciples spent a good part of the 10 days, appears to be a place of peace, quiet and security. Undoubtedly, the Holy Spirit was present there in an unusual way. Much time would have been spent in looking back and thanking Jesus for all that His life and ministry had meant to them.

Times such as these, in warm fellowship with other believers in the presence of God, are precious. Through prayer, we are drawn into a close and fulfilling relationship with the Father. I can imagine that in the Upper Room the disciples were discovering "who we are in Christ." Much time, undoubtedly, was spent in worship and praise, pouring out their souls to "an audience of One." They could have been telling each other that it was a special time of God receiving them as they *are*, not evaluating them by what they *do*. It must have seemed to them as a foretaste of heaven where one day we will all be around God's throne, worshiping Him and exalting His name.

All that for 10 days. But suddenly the "until" took effect and they received the power they had been waiting for. From then on, it was action, ministry and the practical application of the power they had received. Within 24 hours, they had produced 3,000 unpolished disciples of Christ who needed care and nurture in their Christian faith. And the action sparked that day continued for the 30-year span of the book of Acts, having notable pauses, such as the apostles' desire to **give ourselves continually to prayer and to the ministry of the word** (Acts 6:4).

Now, nothing is particularly significant in a period of 10 days. The apostle Paul, who had not been with Jesus personally, needed several years as his tarrying time before God launched him into active ministry. But the point is, we must not allow the time spent in preministry spiritual formation to extend indefinitely. God, I know, does call some to a lifetime of Upper Room style service to Himself, particularly some of those to whom He has given the spiritual gift of intercession. But these might comprise only 5 percent of the Body of Christ, as I explain in my book *Your Spiritual Gifts Can Help Your Church Grow*. I thank God for these intercessors, and feel privileged to know some personally and to count them as personal intercessors for my wife, Doris, and me. They may be relatively few, but they are as important to the Body of Christ as the tiny pituitary gland is to the whole human body.

My concern, however, is for many among the other 95 percent who have fallen into a rut and become what I have heard Doris call "professional tarriers." The tarrying is not optional, it is necessary. If we do not have the intimacy with God, we will not have the power. It is as necessary as food is to the human body. But tarrying, like food, can be overdone. Physical obesity can prevent our bodies from being all that God intends them to be. And spiritual obesity can have similar outcomes. If we do not ever get out of the Upper Room and into the marketplace in Jerusalem and elsewhere, God's plans will thereby be stalled.

Power and Mission

5. ...for John truly baptized with water, but you shall be baptized with the Holy Spirit not many days from now. 6. Therefore, when they had come together, they asked Him, saying, "Lord, will You at this time restore the kingdom to Israel?" 7. And He said to them, "It is not for you to know the times or seasons which the Father has put in His own authority. 8. But you shall receive power when the Holy Spirit has come upon you; and you shall be witnesses to Me in Jerusalem, and in all Judea and Samaria, and to the end of the earth."

....

6. ...will You at this time restore the kingdom to Israel?

....

It continues to be surprising to me that, even after Jesus' death and resurrection, the disciples had not yet comprehended the nature of the kingdom of God. John Stott says it well: "Their question must have filled Jesus with dismay. Were they still so lacking in perception?...the verb restore shows they were expecting a political and territorial kingdom; the noun Israel that they were expecting a national kingdom; and the adverbial clause at this time that they were expecting its immediate establishment."[6]

Sadly, many today seem to have similar concepts of bringing in the Kingdom. Of course it is our Christian duty to strive for justice, righteousness, freedom and prosperity in our society. But some carry this, like tarrying, too far and seem to forget that "the weapons of our warfare are not carnal" (2 Cor. 10:4). And they begin to walk according to the flesh and not the spirit, using force and political coercion to accomplish what they believe to be God's kingdom values. On the contrary, the crucial force for spreading the Kingdom throughout the earth would be the power of the Holy Spirit and personal witness, as Jesus would soon say to them.

The Baptism of the Holy Spirit

....

5. ...you shall be baptized with the Holy Spirit...

....

The spiritual power for advancing the Kingdom would come through the baptism of the Holy Spirit. Unfortunately, differences of understanding what is meant by the baptism of the Holy Spirit have been used by the enemy to separate segments of the Body of Christ for almost 100 years. I am glad to report, however, that former differences are rapidly disappearing from the scene, although it will be some time before they are entirely gone, if ever.

Because of this encouraging trend, I do not regard it necessary to analyze the debate in any depth. Suffice it to say, sincere believers on both sides are seeking the same thing, namely, the unobstructed power of the Holy Spirit in their lives and ministries. I realize that it is more than a semantic issue; nevertheless, a brief look at semantics may help cool the remaining fires of debate somewhat.

Three separate terms are used for the power-bestowing event Luke is describing here:

- **Baptized with the Holy Spirit;**
- **The Holy Spirit has come upon you;**
- **Filled with the Holy Spirit (2:4).**

The verb "baptized" in reference to the Holy Spirit is used only one more time in Acts, when Peter explains that what happened in the house of Cornelius was a fulfillment of Jesus' saying, **John indeed baptized with water, but you shall be baptized with the Holy Spirit** (Acts 11:16).

The verb "filled" with the Holy Spirit is used four other times in Acts. It is used a second time for Peter who was **filled with the Holy Spirit** (Acts 4:8); the believers were again **filled with the Holy Spirit** when they assembled for a prayer meeting (Acts 4:31); Ananias ministered to Saul to be **filled with the Holy Spirit** in Damascus (Acts 9:17); and Paul again was **filled with the Holy Spirit** for his power encounter with Bar-Jesus the sorcerer (Acts 13:9).

The expression "filled with the Holy Spirit" is used only once in the Epistles, where Paul contrasts it to being "drunk with wine" (Eph. 5:18). And, finally, Paul uses "baptized" only once in his Epistles, where he says, "By one Spirit we were all baptized into one body" (1 Cor. 12:13).

Issues such as whether we are baptized or filled with the Spirit once or many times, whether it occurs at conversion or subsequent to conversion, or whether there is initial physical evidence to certify that it has happened, are more important to some Christian leaders today than others. But the reason the issues are raised is a good one: *We need to receive the supernatural power of the Holy Spirit in our lives and our ministries to the greatest extent possible in order to serve God well in our world.*

Receiving the Power for Witnessing

8. ...you shall receive power...and you shall be witnesses to Me...

Acts 1:8 is the fifth appearance of Jesus' Great Commission, following Matthew, "Make disciples of all the nations" (28:19); Mark, "Preach the gospel to every creature" (16:15); Luke, "Repentance and remission of sins should be preached in His name to all nations" (24:47); and John, "As the Father has sent Me, I also send you" (20:21). Four of them, John being the exception, specify the international, global scope of the evangelistic task mandated by Jesus.

On another occasion, Jesus said, "And this gospel of the kingdom will be preached in all the world as a witness to all the nations, and then the end will come" (Matt. 24:14). This seems to indicate that world evangelization is not an endless task, but that it is on a divine time line. The specific goal is to plant the outposts of the kingdom of God, which are principally Christian churches, in every nation or *ethnos*. Today, we would say in every "people group."

As this is being written, missiologists are suggesting for the first time in Christian history that there appears to be light at the end of the Great Commission tunnel! For the first time, there seems to be good reason to believe that the Body of Christ now has the human resources, the material resources and the spiritual resources to complete the task. The A.D. 2000 and Beyond Movement has the faith and hope to believe that it can be done before the end of our present century if only Christians today do what the disciples in Acts did, receive the power and obey the command to witness to the uttermost parts of the earth. Their motto is: "A church for every people and the gospel for every person by the year 2000."

Satan's territory has been shrinking steadily over the centuries since the Acts of the Apostles, but never as rapidly as it has been in the last few decades. Missiologist George Otis Jr. says it as well as any: "The soldiers of the Lord of hosts have now encircled the final strongholds of the serpent—the nations and spiritual principalities of the 10/40 Window. While the remaining task is admittedly the most challenging phase of the battle, the armies of Lucifer are faced presently with a community of believers whose spiritual resources—if properly motivated, submitted and unified—are truly awesome."[7]

The general boundaries of the 10/40 Window, a term coined by missiologist Luis Bush, are shown on the following map:

"10/40 WINDOW"

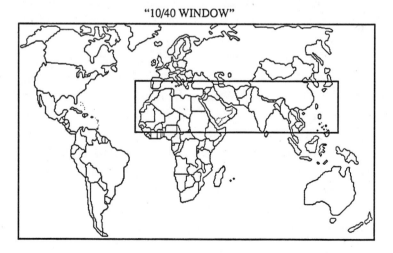

Although I admit it is a broad overgeneralization, the situation today is that a baby born outside the 10/40 Window will have a reasonable chance in its lifetime to hear the gospel of Christ. However, a baby born today within the 10/40 Window will not even hear the gospel of Christ in its lifetime. If the forces of God can achieve a church for every people and the gospel for every person by A.D. 2000, the good news will be that a baby born anywhere in the world that year will have a chance to hear the gospel in its lifetime. When I speak of the end of the Great Commission tunnel, I do not mean everybody in the world will be saved, but that everyone will be within reasonable reach of the gospel. In other words, this gospel of the Kingdom will have been preached to all the world as a witness to all nations!

The most obvious thing about this scenario to sober missiologists is that no human plan or strategy could possibly accomplish the task between now and the year 2000. It can only be done with an extraordinary outpouring of supernatural power through the Holy Spirit. Many believe that if the Iron Curtain could come down, as it did, with such little previous warning, a series of similar events over the next few years could radically change the political landscape of the world and topple some of the most formidable traditional barriers to the gospel.

But, as Otis says, this final thrust will certainly be the most challenging of the battle. Satan is probably more deeply entrenched in the 10/40 Window than he ever has been elsewhere in the world. Spiritual power in the Body of Christ has been increasing rapidly over the past decades as a result of the accumulation of the contributions of the holiness movement, the Pentecostal movement, the social justice movement, the prayer movement, the prophetic movement and, more recently, the spiritual warfare movement. Fresh insights into strategic-level spiritual warfare and spiritual mapping have added what some call new "spiritual technology" to provide the required power boost for this final thrust.

The Keys to the Kingdom

Strategic-level spiritual warfare is one expression of the power given by the Holy Spirit that has been spreading rapidly on all continents over the past few years. As I mentioned in the first chapter, it deals with the principalities and powers described by Paul in Ephesians 6:12. Strategic-level spiritual warfare is somewhat different from ground-level spiritual warfare (casting out demons from individuals) and occult-level spiritual warfare (dealing with witches, curses, New Age channelers and the like). A substantial body of literature has been forthcoming in this relatively new field.[8]

In all probability, part of Jesus' teaching of **things pertaining to the kingdom of God** during the 40 days He was with His disciples, had to do with the keys of the Kingdom, mentioned in Matthew 16:19. The keys, directly related to evangelism ("I will build My church"), contain the power to bind and loose.

Jesus speaks of "binding and loosing" in Matthew 12:29, but a clearer picture of what this involves is found in Luke 11, the parallel passage. Referring to Beelzebub, a principality ranking somewhere near the top of the hierarchy of evil, Jesus says, "When a strong man, fully armed, guards his own palace, his goods are in peace" (Luke 11:21). Obviously, the most prized possession of a ranking principality is unsaved souls. The evangelistic implication is that if the principality's armor remains intact, lost souls will not be saved.

However, it is possible that "a stronger than he comes upon him and overcomes him" (Luke 11:22). When this happens, his armor is ineffective and his spoils, the unsaved souls, can be divided. I take this to mean not that overcoming or binding the strongman saves souls, but it does free them to hear the gospel and make their own decisions about whether to follow Jesus Christ.

Two things are very important here:

1. The word "overcome" (*nikao*) in Luke 11:22, is a parallel expression to "bind" (*deo*) in Matthew 12:29. This indicates that we have here a direct application of the use of the keys of the Kingdom, "Whatever you bind on earth will be bound in heaven" (Matt. 16:19), with presumed evangelistic results.

2. The "stronger than he" cannot be a human being, but it must refer to the "finger of God," or the Holy Spirit, that Jesus said He relied upon to cast a demon out of a mute man in the same passage (see Luke 11:20). But where is the Holy Spirit? He is in believers who have been filled with the Holy Spirit. This power from the Holy Spirit has a direct relationship to Jesus' ascension. Let's look at it.

Are We Better Off Without Jesus?

....

9. Now when He had spoken these things, while they watched, He was taken up, and a cloud received Him out of their sight.

....

This event, called the Ascension, officially ended Jesus' incarnation and His first coming to earth. He will not appear in person to the world again until His second coming.

During His lifetime, particularly near the end, Jesus attempted as best as He could to prepare His disciples for His leaving them. They loved Him so much, it was not easy for them to accept the fact that He would go away and leave them alone. Peter at one point was so upset that he rebuked Jesus and said, "Far be it from You, Lord; this shall not happen to You!" (Matt. 16:22). But Jesus sharply reprimanded him and said, "Get behind Me, Satan! You are an offense to Me" (Matt. 16:23).

Later, Jesus calmly explained to them, "It is to your advantage that I go away" (John 16:7). How could this be? How could anything be an advantage over being with Jesus personally? Very simple. Jesus told them that if He went away, only then could He send the Comforter, the Holy Spirit, who would be with them from then on. It would be to their advantage to be with the Holy Spirit rather than to be with the Son of God. In that case, they would be better off without Jesus than with Him in person.

One of the advantages of having the Holy Spirit would be that they would have access to the only power source capable of binding or overcoming the strongmen who are out there keeping entire people groups in spiritual darkness.

For the most part, the disciples were ready for Jesus' exit and by then they had understood it fairly well. Still, they were somewhat stupefied when He actually ascended into heaven from the Mount of Olives, and they stared into the clouds so long that two angels had to come to move them along:

> 11. Who also said, "Men of Galilee, why do you stand gazing up into heaven? This same Jesus, who was taken up from you into heaven, will so come in like manner as you saw Him go into heaven."

This brought the disciples back to their senses, and they went to Jerusalem where they joined history's most powerful prayer meeting.

History's Most Powerful Prayer Meeting

12. Then they returned to Jerusalem from the Mount

> called Olivet, which is near Jerusalem, a Sabbath day's
> journey. 13. And when they had entered, they went up
> into the upper room where they were staying:...
> 14. These all continued with one accord in prayer and
> supplication, with the women and Mary the mother of
> Jesus, and with His brothers. 15. ...(altogether the
> number of names was about a hundred and twenty).

....

We need to go back to Luke's Gospel momentarily to get the whole picture. In Acts, we see that the disciples were meeting for prayer in the Upper Room, but, during these 10 days, they also "were continually in the temple praising and blessing God" (Luke 24:53). This combination of praise and worship with sincere prayer and supplication is an unbeatable formula for drawing near to God, opening ourselves to the fullness of the Holy Spirit and hearing the voice of the Father.

Ten days in prayer is a very long prayer meeting. Most of us, including myself, would have a hard time trying to block out 10 straight days for worship and prayer. As I have been participating in coordinating the worldwide prayer movement, however, I have come into contact with some who are doing such things. A recent two-week event for prayer only was held in Australia, for example. Some, particularly orders of nuns, cloister themselves for a lifetime of prayer. Prayer summits of four days each are becoming popular in many cities of the United States and elsewhere, and Christian leaders who participate in them regard having done it as a fairly heroic spiritual accomplishment. But this was not 4 days in the Jerusalem Upper Room, it was 10 days.

The agenda of the prayer meeting had been set by the Lord: "Tarry...until you are endued with power from on high" (Luke 24:49). They were regrouping to begin the process of world evangelization, and they knew from the outset that the task was one that required extraordinary spiritual power. There is no indication that they knew the prayer meeting would last for 10 days. They only knew it was **not many days from now** (Acts 1:5), so they had settled in for the long haul. They engaged in *persistent* prayer, and they were prepared to pray the process through until they knew beyond the shadow of doubt that God had responded.

Would God have responded if they had decided to take a break, after all the stress and strain they had been through, and lay out on the beach at Joppa for a few days? This is not a superficial question, because it raises the issue of whether prayer has anything to do with God's actions. I personally believe that if the disciples had vacationed in Joppa or had gone fishing in the Sea of Galilee instead of spending their time in the Temple and the Upper Room, Pentecost, as we know it, would not have come.

I realize that some who hold a very high view of God's sovereignty might say that prayer doesn't change God; it only changes us. And there is a great deal of theological validity in that. God is infinite, eternal and unchangeable. His nature cannot be changed. And certainly the time in the Upper Room worked a deep and significant change in the disciples themselves. But our sovereign God many times has said things such as, "Call to Me, and I will answer you, and show you great and mighty things, which you do not know" (Jer. 33:3). This sounds very much as though God, in His sovereign wisdom, has so arranged reality that, although He might *desire* to do some things, He *will not* do them unless, and until, Christian people are obedient and faithful in their prayer lives. The whole world has been ultimately blessed because the disciples in Jerusalem decided to be obedient to their Lord and give themselves to prayer.

Not only were the disciples persistent and obedient, but they were also unified. They **continued with one accord**. One reason corporate prayer is often more effective than solitary prayer is the principle of agreement. Jesus said, "If two of you agree on earth concerning anything that they ask, it will be done for them by My Father in heaven" (Matt. 18:19). The prayer of one person alone is certainly not wasted, but the prayer of two in agreement is better, and presumably the prayer of 120 in agreement is better yet.

In practice, prayer evangelism efforts for cities, if they are to have any lasting effect, must begin with the visible unity of the Christian leaders, especially the pastors, in prayer. This is so difficult to accomplish, it is widely recognized as a prime target used by the enemy to prevent the kingdom of God from coming to a given city in any significant and tangible way. Knowing the "devices" of Satan, we can thereby prevent him from taking advantage of us, as Paul says in 2 Corinthians 2:11.

The Wider Nucleus of Believers

14. ...with the women and Mary the mother of Jesus,
and with His brothers. 26. ...and the lot fell on Matthias.
And he was numbered with the eleven apostles.

The women disciples of Jesus do not first enter the picture here, but they are seen as a key component of His ministry team throughout. Who were they? We do not know the names of many of them, but some we do know. "And certain women who had been healed of evil spirits and infirmities—Mary called Magdalene, out of whom had come seven demons, and Joanna the wife of Chuza, Herod's steward, and Susanna, and many others who provided for Him from their substance" (Luke 8:2,3). Among other things, these faithful women covered what was probably a substantial part of Jesus' ministry expenses.

Jesus' mother, Mary, was also there, and this is the last time she appears in Scripture. There is some debate, particularly from

Roman Catholic theologians who hold to the doctrine of the perpetual virginity of Mary, whether Jesus' "brothers" were blood brothers. Most interpreters, however, take the Greek word *adelphoi* to mean natural children of Mary and Joseph. His brothers did not believe in Jesus during His ministry time, as we read in John 7:5, although by the Day of Pentecost they had become disciples. They are identified by name in Mark 6:3: "Is this not the carpenter, the Son of Mary, and brother of James, Joses, Judas, and Simon?"

It will be important for us later on to recognize here that those among the 12 apostles named James, Judas and Simon (Peter), and Simon the Zealot were different people; they were not from Jesus' own family. Later on, however, we find that "James" becomes the leader of the Jerusalem church. This is not the apostle James, but James the brother of Jesus who also writes the Epistle of James.

The leadership of the nucleus of believers was brought once again up to 12 apostles when Matthias was chosen to replace Judas. Some, for a variety of reasons, feel that this could have been a precipitous decision taken under the pressure of one of Peter's well-known impulses. But it seems to me that if their 10 days of praise, worship, prayer and supplication were all they appear to be, the disciples would have been closely enough in touch with the Father to have known His will for Matthias.

More than anything else, however, it was the dramatic answer to prayer we see in the next chapter that qualifies this as "history's most powerful prayer meeting."

Reflection Questions

1. Do you think it makes sense to say that theology emerges from ministry and not the other way around? Why?
2. Discuss the concept that Jesus ministered on earth through

His human nature by the power of the Holy Spirit. Does that mean He was not God during His incarnation?

3. Can you name others who have shifted their paradigms toward accepting supernatural signs and wonders in ways similar to Charles Kraft or Jack Deere or Peter Wagner?

4. Do you share the concern that some Christians tend to be "professional tarriers" and spend a disproportionate amount of their time and energy in enjoying their personal relationship to God while scarcely getting around to moving out and sharing God's love with others?

5. What is your personal view of the "baptism of the Holy Spirit"? How does this relate to being "filled with the Holy Spirit"?

Notes

1. Ken Blue, *Authority to Heal* (Downers Grove, IL: InterVarsity Press, 1987).

2. Don Williams, *Signs, Wonders and the Kingdom of God* (Ann Arbor, MI: Servant Publications, 1989).

3. Ray S. Anderson, ed., *Theological Foundations for Ministry* (Grand Rapids, MI: William B. Eerdmans Publishing Co., 1979), p. 7. Used by permission.

4. Colin Brown, *That You May Believe: Miracles and Faith Then and Now* (Grand Rapids, MI: William B. Eerdmans Publishing Co., 1985), p. 97.

5. Thomas A. Smail, *Reflected Glory: The Spirit in Christ and in Christians* (London, England: Hodder and Stoughton, 1975), p. 70.

6. John R. W. Stott, *The Spirit, the Church and the World: The Message of Acts* (Downers Grove, IL: InterVarsity Press, 1990), p. 41.

7. George Otis Jr., *The Last of the Giants* (Grand Rapids, MI: Fleming H. Revell Company, a division of Baker Book House Company, 1991), p. 144.

8. Some of the literature dealing with strategic-level spiritual warfare includes John Dawson, *Taking Our Cities for God* (Altamonte Springs, FL:

Creation House, 1989); Cindy Jacobs, *Possessing the Gates of the Enemy* (Grand Rapids, MI: Fleming H. Revell Company, 1991); George Otis Jr., *The Last of the Giants* (Grand Rapids, MI: Fleming H. Revell Company, 1991); Francis Frangipane, *The House of the Lord* (Altamonte Springs, FL: Creation House, 1991); and three contributions of mine: *Engaging the Enemy, Warfare Prayer and Breaking Strongholds in Your City*, all published by Regal Books.

CHAPTER

4

Acts 2

The Spiritual Explosion at Pentecost

Acts 2
The Holy Spirit Comes in Power

1. Now when the Day of Pentecost had fully come,
   they were all with one accord in one place.
2. And suddenly there came a sound from heaven,
   as of a rushing mighty wind, and it filled the
   whole house where they were sitting.
3. Then there appeared to them divided tongues,
   as of fire, and one sat upon each of them.
4. And they were all filled with the Holy Spirit
   and began to speak with other tongues,
   as the Spirit gave them utterance.

Pentecost—The Harvest Festival

....

1. Now when the Day of Pentecost had fully come.

....

"Pentecost" is the Greek word for "fiftieth." It marked the annual Jewish festival scheduled for 50 days after the Passover. It was called the Feast of Weeks, but also the Feast of Harvest, because on that day Jewish people presented to the Lord the firstfruits of the annual wheat harvest (see Exod. 34:22).

Was it a coincidence that the Holy Spirit would bring the power the disciples needed for being witnesses to Jesus in Jerusalem, Judea, Samaria and to the uttermost parts of the earth precisely on the day designated for Jews to lift their thanks to Jehovah God for the harvest? Possibly, but I don't think so.

The disciples were about to begin reaping a harvest of souls that has continued now for almost 2,000 years. Jesus had said to His disciples, "Behold, I say to you, lift up your eyes and look at the fields, for they are already white for harvest! And he who reaps receives wages, and gathers fruit for eternal life" (John 4:35,36). Jesus had also said, "The harvest truly is plentiful, but the laborers are few. Therefore pray the Lord of the harvest to send out laborers into His harvest" (Matt. 9:37,38).

What were the disciples praying for **with one accord in one place?** They were praying for the Holy Spirit to come upon them and impart to them the power needed for carrying the gospel across all conceivable barriers. They were praying that God would send them forth as laborers into the harvest fields of the day.

It is good missionary strategy to develop what Donald McGavran calls "a theology of harvest." McGavran is impatient with missionaries and evangelists who are satisfied with searching for the lost with little or no regard for how many are ultimately found. Too many Christian workers have seen such little fruit for their labors that, McGavran says, they "had to find a rationale for existence and continuance that did not depend on numbers or converts." They would say, "Results should not be used to evaluate success or failure."[1]

Fortunately, the disciples in the Upper Room knew nothing of such a "search theology." They were praying for something much more positive. They knew that Jesus had come to save the lost, and they knew that God's intent was, as McGavran so forcefully puts it, "to marshall, discipline, strengthen, and multiply His churches until all people on earth have had the chance to hear the gospel from their own kindred, who speak their own language and whose word is unobstructed by cultural barriers."[2] This is a theology of harvest that was as valid then as it is now.

Visible Signs of the Invisible Spirit

Presumably, all 120 were together in some house when their prayers were finally answered and the Holy Spirit came. We are not sure whether the house was the Upper Room, or perhaps some other house in the Temple grounds, because they were spending time daily in each place. Because of the large space that would have been needed to accommodate the crowd that gathered, it was most likely a structure connected with the Temple.

Again, **they were all with one accord**, a phrase repeated, significantly in my opinion, from Acts 1:14 to remind us of the need for spiritual agreement in prayer as a prerequisite for receiving optimum spiritual power.

When the Holy Spirit came, there was no room for doubt that it was a unique occasion. Nothing like this had happened when Jesus, the second Person of the Trinity, was on earth with His disciples. God showed them clearly what He meant when He said that it would be to their *advantage* to have the Holy Spirit with them instead of the Son. Three tangible signs indicated that the Holy Spirit had come:

> **2. And suddenly there came a sound from heaven, as of a rushing mighty wind,...**

The sound must have been tremendous. Those who live in areas that do not experience windstorms or tornadoes or hurricanes may not appreciate the volume of sound from strong winds. There was no indication that an unusual meteorological wind was actually blowing at the time. But we should not miss the possible significance of wind, even if only its sound, being used as an analogy for the Holy Spirit, as in John 3:8: "The wind blows where it wishes,...So is everyone who is born of the Spirit." The sound apparently was public and external, not just some phenomenon of group psychology only the believers had experienced. It was loud enough, unusual enough and probably terrifying enough, so that people in the Temple area of Jerusalem, or from other parts of the city as well, were drawn toward it to see what strange thing might be happening (see Acts 2:6). In our day, it would have made the 6:00 P.M. news.

> **3. ...there appeared to them divided tongues, as of fire, and one sat upon each of them.**

The first tangible sign was audible, the second was visual. At presumably the same time they heard the sound of wind, the disciples actually saw 120 separate fires shaped like tongues resting on one another. At that moment, few would have had to be reminded of John the Baptist's prophecy concerning Jesus: "He will baptize you with the Holy Spirit and with fire" (Luke 3:16).

Those familiar with the Old Testament knew well how fire was often used by God to give tangible evidence of His power, His presence and His holiness. The climax of the great power encounter between Elijah and the priests of Baal was fire. "The fire of the Lord fell and consumed the burnt sacrifice, and the wood and the stones and the dust, and it licked up the water that was in the trench" (1 Kings 18:38). Moses experienced God's presence in the burning bush (see Exod. 3:2), and Isaiah's lips were touched with a burning coal of holiness from the altar (see Isa. 6:6,7). Nothing could be more indicative of the need for each person who is to be used by God for world evangelization to experience His power, live in His presence and be characterized by His holiness. These were all included in the Promise of the Father (Acts 1:4).

---

4. And they...began to speak with other tongues,...

The third tangible sign was oral. Few things could be more surprising to human beings than suddenly speaking in a language they did not learn. When the Holy Spirit came, the disciples immediately experienced the first fulfillment of Jesus' prophetic word to them: "Most assuredly, I say to you, he who believes in Me, the works that I do he will do also; and greater works than these he will do, because I go to My Father" (John 14:12).

Some have trouble with the "greater works" part of this promise. They ask how anyone could do greater works than Jesus Christ. The answer lies in the fact, as I have previously explained, that the power by which Jesus did His works was the Holy Spirit, and that the power through which Jesus' disciples do their works is the same Holy Spirit, who is God Himself and who can do works of any magnitude at any time He wishes. If we relied on human power to do our works, none of us could even approach any of Jesus' works. But our works can be done with superhuman power, provided by God Himself.

To me it is notable that the first miracle recorded after Jesus' ascension is a work that, as far as we know, the Holy Spirit never did through Jesus. Jesus never spoke in a language He didn't learn. But the disciples did. In fact, among them, they spoke in at least 15 other tongues and were understood by those who spoke them as their native languages. Whether this is a *greater* work can be debated. But it surely was vastly *different* from anything that had happened before.

In my international travels, I hear from time to time how this miracle is occurring today. For some time, I recorded the instances that were reported to me by credible witnesses, but I no longer do that. Not that this miraculous gift of language has become routine (I did not receive it when I went to Bolivia as a missionary), but it is frequent enough to no longer be particularly surprising. I did spend some personal time with American missionaries to Argentina, James and Jaime Thomas, who themselves instantly received the Spanish language, including an Argentine accent, while in the city of Cordoba. Several other instances are documented in my book *How to Have a Healing Ministry in Any Church* (pp. 157-160).

The Amazed Unbelievers

5. Now there were dwelling in Jerusalem Jews,
devout men, from every nation under heaven.
6. And when this sound occurred, the multitude came
together, and were confused, because everyone heard them
speak in his own language. 7. Then they were all amazed
and marveled, saying to one another, "Look, are not all
these who speak Galileans? 8. And how is it that we hear,

each in our own language in which we were born?"
13. Others mocking said, "They are full of new wine."

Who were these Jews in Jerusalem?

Coming **from every nation under heaven** (an obvious literary exaggeration, because none came from Japan or Aborigine Australia or Tibet) refers to the nations of the first-century Jewish dispersion. These Jews, who lived with their families in Jewish communities outside of the Holy Land, ordinarily anchored by a local synagogue, were known as Hellenistic Jews. In the society of that day, they were clearly distinguished from the *Hebrew* Jews who did live in the Holy Land. For most, their heart language would have been the vernacular of the city or province or nation where they were born and raised and where they did most of their business. Those who came from lands to the west and north of Palestine would also know Greek, the trade language of the Roman Empire in those days. In fact, the word "Hellenistic" means that they were molded to some degree by Greek culture.

Missiologically speaking, the Hellenists would ordinarily be regarded as a people group distinct from the Hebrews, and therefore, reaching them would require E-2 evangelism. To complicate matters further, their various identities with certain Roman provinces or cities or republics or nations outside Roman jurisdiction such as Iran (Parthians) or Iraq (Mesopotamia), as well as their own particular heart languages, would divide them into many significant subgroups.

Luke lists 15 language groups in Acts 2:9-11, but there is no reason to assume that this is a complete list as opposed to a representative list. It seems strange, for example, that none are mentioned from Greece or Syria. The Jewish Talmud reported that there were 70 nations in the Jewish dispersion, and because Luke says they had come **from every nation under heaven,** it could be that many more than 15 language groups were represented.

Although most of them would be Hellenistic Jews, a number of them were also **proselytes,** according to verse 10. The proselytes were Gentiles by birth, but they had decided to convert to Judaism and had gone through the prescribed rituals that included baptism and circumcision for the males.

Why Were There So Many in Jerusalem?

It is not known exactly how many inhabitants Jerusalem had in the time of Jesus. Joachim Jeremias, a specialist on the social conditions of Jerusalem in the first century, estimates the population to be somewhere around 25,000 or 30,000. But then he says, "There can be no doubt that the influx of pilgrims at Passover time from all over the world was immense, and amounted to several times the population of Jerusalem."[3] Passover, however, was only one of three major Jewish festivals that annually attracted large numbers of pilgrims. Passover was held in early spring, Pentecost came 50 days later, then the Feast of the Tabernacles took place each fall. Of the three, Pentecost had the advantage of occurring during the most ideal weather period in the eastern Mediterranean region, and it may well have been the annual festival that attracted the most visitors.

On the Day of Pentecost, when the Holy Spirit came, 100,000 Hellenists would easily have been visiting Jerusalem, possibly 200,000.

The First Attempt at E-2 Evangelism

....

8. And how is it that we hear, each in our own
language in which we were born?

....

From the time Jesus was baptized to this point, virtually all the evangelism recorded in the Bible was monocultural, or E-1 evangelism. This is an extremely significant passage because it is the first time in the New Testament record that the disciples took the gospel across a significant cultural barrier and engaged in cross-cultural or E-2 evangelism.

Even if the Holy Spirit had come upon the disciples with fire in the Upper Room, by now they must have been located in the Temple area because of the **multitude** that gathered. This first public evangelistic service could have attracted tens of thousands of people, as do many such services today.

Although they were all Jews, the gap between the Hebrews and the Hellenists was formidable. For example, only in rare exceptions, such as business associates, would they even spend a social evening together any more than in the Ramadan pilgrimage to Mecca, Indonesian Muslims today would socialize with Saudi Arabian Muslims. The Elamites who were there in Jerusalem, for example, were from families that never had returned to Palestine from the Babylonian captivity but, rather, had settled down in the area north of the Persian Gulf, part of the Persian empire, but with their own vernacular language as well. They, like the Hebrew Jews, might have been descendants of Abraham, but they would have very little in common with each other except to mingle impersonally in crowds, such as gathered at the Temple when the sound of rushing mighty wind drew them there.

To further highlight the drama of this event, I will repeat that not only were virtually all of the believers up to this time Hebrews as opposed to Hellenists, but also the vast majority, including all the leadership, were *Galilean* Hebrews as opposed to *Judean* Hebrews. They were the hillbillies of the day, regarded as culturally backward by many Judeans and undoubtedly by the

Hellenists as well. But the Galileans were the evangelists, the instruments chosen by God to take the good news that the Messiah had come to Hellenists from all over the world. To draw a present-day parallel among white, European-Americans, it would be roughly equivalent to West Virginia coal miners attempting to evangelize the Massachusetts Institute of Technology (MIT) alumni association. One of the first things that would predictably turn off the MIT graduates would be what they would consider the evangelists' ungrammatical Appalachian accent.

Contextualizing the Gospel

The apostles could have preached to the crowd in the Temple in Aramaic and communicated fairly well. Those among them who might have known Greek could have done the same. But God had other plans to cross what we now see as a formidable cultural barrier. He did something that has not established a missiological pattern, but it is a principle. God took steps to contextualize the gospel, thereby showing that He respects the culture and language of each of the multiple groups gathered there. The method He used was to perform a miracle of language and allow the disciples to speak in languages they had never learned.

The first principle of cross-cultural evangelism is to present the message of Christ in cultural forms appropriate to the new people group. Today's missionaries would not feel adequately equipped if they were not steeped in cultural anthropology and did not have the tools to distinguish what is a nonnegotiable part of the Christian faith from cultural baggage they might unconsciously be carrying along with them as foreigners. Early missionaries to Africa, for example, in many cases retarded the spread of the gospel due to some culturally biased decisions concerning polygamy. In parts of Asia, missionary rules relating to ancestor worship often went beyond what true biblical requirements would be. But these are some of the advanced issues in contextualization. More basic would be the common agreement that if people of other cultures are going to be evangelized effectively, the gospel must be preached in their heart language, and the Bible must be translated into their vernacular.

Resistance and Receptivity

> 12. So they were all amazed... 13. Others mocking said, "They are full of new wine."

Ordinarily, when the gospel is preached to unbelievers, some accept it and some reject it. Some are receptive and some are resistant. To return to the harvest analogy, not all crops ripen at the same time. Even the same crop does not all ripen at once, as we know from the annual United States wheat harvest in which the wheat in the southern states ripens before the wheat in the northern states. Where do the harvesters go? They naturally go where the harvest is ripe, not where it is still green.

The disciples at Pentecost knew this because Jesus had previously demonstrated it for them. When He first sent them out on their own to the "lost sheep of the house of Israel" (Matt. 10:6), He told them to research each city to find "who in it is worthy, and stay there till you go out" (Matt. 10:11). These are the receptive, the whitened harvest. And the resistant? "Whoever will not receive you nor hear your words, when you depart from that house or city, shake off the dust from your feet" (Matt. 10:14).

We see both kinds at Pentecost. Those who were receptive recognized the extraordinary miracle of languages. They said,

"Aren't these people those hillbilly Galileans?" (see Acts 2:7). They knew that in no human way could such uneducated people speak in Egyptian or Arabic or Persian, but that was exactly what they were doing! They knew it could only have been done by supernatural power, and they sincerely wanted to know more about it. They said, **"Whatever could this mean?"** (2:12).

But the resistant were also there. Although they were personally witnessing the miraculous power of God, they refused to acknowledge it as such. They accused the apostles of being drunk, even though they must have known in calmer moments that one of the recognized phenomena of drunkenness is not beginning to speak in languages one has never learned. Even though the noise of the wind and speaking in unknown tongues should have impressed them, because, as Paul says, "For Jews request a sign" (1 Cor. 1:22), they remained indifferent. They are a prime example of the god of this age blinding the minds of those who do not believe (see 2 Cor. 4:4).

Speaking in Tongues

Speaking in tongues will surface several times again as we move through Acts, so it may be helpful to discuss the issues involved in some detail at this point and simply refer back to them later.

Although the phenomenon of speaking in tongues can be found from time to time in the history of the Christian Church, it never mainstreamed throughout the universal Body of Christ as it has in the twentieth century. The event that seemed to spark the modern tongues movement occurred during a New Year's Eve service in Topeka, Kansas, beginning on December 31, 1900, and ending on January 1, 1901, precisely the first day of the twentieth century. The prophetic symbolism of the day itself has not been lost to historians who have traced the subsequent tongues movement and observed its virtual universality 100 years later.

But this did not come without opposition. The Pentecostal movement that emerged from Topeka, and later the Azusa Street revival in Los Angeles, was resisted as well as scorned by more traditional Christians. Pentecostals were listed by some theologians as a false cult, along with Jehovah's Witnesses and Christian Scientists. The German Lutheran Church issued a "Berlin Declaration," stating that the power exhibited by Pentecostals was from below, not from above. Because many of them were from a social class similar to first-century Galileans, the tongues speakers were scorned as "Holy Rollers" or as practicing the "hillbilly religion."

After the middle of the century, however, diplomatic Pentecostal leaders, such as David du Plessis and Thomas Zimmerman, guided the tongues-speaking movement into fellowship with more mainstream evangelicalism, with the World Council of Churches as well as with the Vatican. The process gained momentum through the appearance of the charismatic movement and then the Third Wave. Now, the most rapidly growing segment of Christianity worldwide, known by many as "postdenominationalism," regards speaking in tongues as a common, but not a necessary, part of Christian life. Some postdenominational churches use tongues extensively, others discourage it and most are in between. To none is speaking in tongues any longer a serious or divisive issue.

The Gift of Tongues

Except for a diminishing number of Christians who are holding out for a cessationist theology, supposing that the more dramatic miraculous gifts of the Spirit ceased with the close of the Apostolic Age, there is widespread agreement that speaking in tongues is a bona fide gift of the Holy Spirit found among believers today.

"Different kinds of tongues" as well as "interpretation of tongues" are listed as spiritual gifts in 1 Corinthians 12:10. In my book *Your Spiritual Gifts Can Help Your Church Grow*, I define it as follows:

> The gift of tongues is the special ability that God gives to certain members of the Body of Christ (A) to speak to God in a language they have never learned and/or (B) to receive and communicate an immediate message of God to His people through a divinely anointed utterance in a language they have never learned.[4]

Notice that tongues can either be private, between the individual and God, or public, directed to the congregation as a whole. Private tongues are described by the apostle Paul in these words: "He who speaks in a tongue does not speak to men but to God, for no one understands him" (1 Cor. 14:2). Paul places no restrictions on the use of private tongues, but he does on public tongues. They must be used only when accompanied by interpretation, otherwise "you will be speaking into the air" (1 Cor. 14:9). He adds, "Therefore let him who speaks in a tongue pray that he may interpret" (1 Cor. 14:13). Public tongues plus interpretation are regarded as the equivalent of prophecy, although Paul prefers prophecy (see 1 Cor. 14:5 and 39).

A Miracle of Languages

Were the tongues spoken on Pentecost the gift of tongues or something else? I agree with Simon Kistemaker who says, "We cannot equate the Pentecost event with tongue speaking in the Corinthian church....Whereas in the Corinthian church ecstatic speech has to be interpreted, at Pentecost the hearers do not need interpreters because they hear and are able to understand in their own languages."[5] I think that what happened at Pentecost was more of a "miracle of languages" than a "gift of tongues."

This is not to imply that the spiritual gift of tongues is never a true human language that at the time neither the speaker nor the hearers can identify. Sometimes it is. On a recent visit to England, for example, I learned of an incident where a monolingual British pastor was ministering to a multilingual Arab who happened to be serving as the principal translator in England for the OPEC oil cartel. The pastor sensed that God wanted him to pray about a certain physical ailment that the Muslim was suffering, and as he did so, he prayed some in tongues, as was his custom. The Arab was amazed, just as were the unbelievers on Pentecost. The pastor had first prayed in fluent Iranian, then later in fluent Ugaritic, an obsolete language! The meaning of the prayers in the two different languages was identical. In this case, the Arab acknowledged it as a miracle of God, was born again, and is now a strong witness among fellow Muslims.

On the other hand, some social scientists, fascinated with the phenomenon of *glossalalia*, to use the Greek term, have tape-recorded tongue speaking and submitted it to analysis of professional linguists. Their conclusion is that the speech they examined follows no known human language structure, ancient or modern. The difference between these two instances might be what Paul referred to when he said, "Though I speak with the tongues of men and of angels" (1 Cor. 13:1). Some apparently are human languages, some are not.

Tongues and the Pentecost Event

I use the term "Pentecost event," because I believe these initial stages of world evangelization were so crucial that two other occasions also recorded in Acts should join the outpouring of the Holy Spirit on the Day of Pentecost as equal parts of a total "Pentecost event." All three were barrier-breaking milestones:

- Breaking the barrier between Hebrew Jews and

Hellenistic Jews in Jerusalem on the day of Pentecost (see Acts 2).

- Breaking the barrier between Jews and Samaritans through Philip in Samaria (see Acts 8:5-25).
- Breaking the barrier between Jews and Gentiles through Peter in the house of Cornelius (see Acts 10).

Through this three-part event, the groundwork had been laid for the spread of the gospel to Jerusalem, Judea, Samaria and to the end of the earth, as Jesus had commanded in Acts 1:8.

In each of the three cases, the Holy Spirit came in power, indicating that the gospel would be spread only through the combination of supernatural intervention and human obedience to God. Two were accompanied with the phenomenon of tongues, and one was not:

- At Pentecost, **...they were all filled with the Holy Spirit and began to speak with other tongues, as the Spirit gave them utterance** (Acts 2:4).
- In Samaria, **...they laid hands on them, and they received the Holy Spirit** (Acts 8:17). No mention is made of tongues.
- In Cornelius' house, **...the Holy Spirit fell upon all those who heard the word. For they heard them speak with tongues and magnify God** (Acts 10:44,46).

Some Christian leaders, who have a more universal view of tongues in the Body of Christ than I, will assume that, although tongues was not mentioned concerning Samaria, the believers must have spoken in tongues because they did so at Pentecost and in Cornelius's house. One of these is Pentecostal scholar Stanley Horton, who says, "The fact that Luke does not mention speaking in tongues here is not significant," and then goes on to affirm that the thing that must have caught the attention of

Simon the sorcerer in Samaria must have been the Samaritans speaking in tongues.[6] Horton could be right, but we must keep in mind that an argument from silence on one side tends to neutralize an argument from silence on the other. I personally do not think it makes much difference whether they spoke in tongues or not. The principal issue, in my mind, is that the Holy Spirit came with power, and the barrier between Jews and Samaritans was broken down.

Peter's Anointed Sermon

....

14. But Peter, standing up with the eleven, raised his voice and said to them, "Men of Judea and all who dwell in Jerusalem, let this be known to you, and heed my words. 36. Therefore let all the house of Israel know assuredly that God has made this Jesus, whom you crucified, both Lord and Christ."

....

After the sound, the fire and hearing the gospel in their own languages from the mouths of a motley group of Galileans, many were ready to learn what all this was about. They had asked, **"Whatever could this mean?"** (Acts 2:12), and now they were about to know. Peter takes leadership here; the other 11 are near him and add their encouragement and approval. Peter also had taken leadership in the Upper Room when they appointed Matthias as the twelfth apostle. Peter is the central character in the book of Acts through chapter 8; he appears several times more through chapter 12; then Paul becomes Luke's central figure for the rest of the book. Meanwhile, James, the natural brother of Jesus and not the James of the original 12, replaces Peter as the leader of the Jerusalem church by the time of the Jerusalem Council in chapter 15.

What language did Peter use to address the multitude? He came from Bethsaida (see John 1:44), which means "Fisherman's City," right on the border of Gentile territory. He would probably, therefore, know Greek as a trade language, but likely with a fluency similar to that of English fluency of many Mexicans who live near the United States border. Just as most such Mexicans would be more comfortable in Spanish, so Peter would undoubtedly have been more comfortable in his native Aramaic, a first cousin of the Hebrew language, which was no longer in widespread use.

The reason I refer to Peter's message as "anointed" is not just because of its unusual results, but also because of the Greek word used for the English said to them in Acts 2:14. Our English versions hide this, but the word derives from *apophthengesthai*, which means "to address someone enthusiastically," according to *The New International Dictionary of New Testament Theology*.[7] This is the same word previously used in 2:4 when the disciples began to speak in tongues and the Holy Spirit gave them utterance. This message of Peter's, like the speaking in tongues, was not something to be explained by skills of human rhetoric or oratory—hardly expected of a Galilean fisherman—but only by divine anointing.

What Did Pentecost Mean?

....

15. For these are not drunk, as you suppose,...
16. But this is what was spoken by the prophet Joel.

....

Peter launches his sermon by using two points of contact with his audience. The first is the stupid accusation that the disciples were drunk, with the sarcastic retort that, as *The Living Bible* puts it, **Some of you are saying these men are drunk! It isn't true!**

It's much too early for that! People don't get drunk by 9 a.m.! The second point of contact was a reference to the Prophet Joel, a spiritual authority for everyone in his audience, whether Hebrew or Hellenist.

Informed Jews would have known from Joel that the "last days" would be marked by some kind of outpouring of God's Spirit, but until seeing the things that had happened that day and hearing Peter's application, they would have had no idea that it had actually begun. The "last days" means that period of time between Jesus' first coming and His second coming. It is the period of time in which we live today. No one knows when Jesus' second coming will take place, but we do know for sure that it is 2,000 years nearer than it was on the Day of Pentecost. We also know, as I have said, that the Great Commission, for the first time since Pentecost, could possibly be completed in our generation.

This, I believe, is why the spiritual warfare related to world evangelization is escalating so rapidly and becoming more intense than it has been in the past. The book of Revelation says, "For the devil has come down to you, having great wrath, because he knows that he has a short time" (Rev. 12:12). I would not be surprised if this prophecy were being fulfilled before our very eyes. The "last days" are not forever. They are on a time line, and it might well be that we are nearing the end, although I am not about to set any dates for the Second Coming. Everyone who has tried it so far has been wrong!

What I desire to stress are the stated characteristics of these "last days":
- The outpouring of the Holy Spirit;
- Prophecy;
- Visions and dreams;
- Signs and wonders;
- Salvation to those who believe.

This is what Pentecost meant then, and it is what larger and larger segments of the Body of Christ are discovering and applying to our evangelistic task today. Power ministries are helping open people's minds in China, in South Africa, in Brazil and in many other nations of the world today. The "last days" are continuing, and Joel's prophecy is continuing to be fulfilled.

The Heart of the Gospel

Signs and wonders do not save people. Neither do prophecy or visions and dreams. Only the gospel of Christ "is the power of God to salvation for everyone who believes" (Rom. 1:16). That is why Peter, in his message, carefully outlines the story of Jesus of Nazareth in the following Acts references:

- Jesus' life and ministry on earth (see 2:22);
- Jesus' crucifixion (see 2:23);
- Jesus' resurrection from the dead (see 2:24-32);
- Jesus' exaltation at the right hand of God (see 2:33-35);
- Jesus, the Christ or the Jewish Messiah (see 2:36).

We want to keep reminding ourselves that ministry in the miraculous power of the Holy Spirit is not primarily an end in itself, but a means toward the end of making disciples. Disciples are made only through a personal relationship to Jesus Christ as Lord and Savior.

Peter drove his words home by accusing his listeners of making a huge mistake by crucifying the very person whom God had sent as their Messiah to save them. It must have taken incredible courage to make such a direct application, but under the anointing of God it turned out to be appropriate. Many in the audience were ready to confess that they had taken Jesus **by lawless hands** (2:23) and crucified Him (see 2:36).

The People Respond with Open Hearts

....

37. ...Men and brethren, what shall we do?

....

The convicting power of the Holy Spirit had come upon them and hearts were opened. Peter responded by giving them two action steps:

Repentance. Repentance means turning away from sin, changing the mind, turning toward God. This is what is needed to become a disciple of Jesus. It is establishing a personal relationship with Jesus through faith.

It is notable that Peter did not pile upon his listeners a list of ethical demands to which they had to agree before they could be saved. Some, today, have the tendency to superimpose their own ethical agendas on the gospel, and they thereby hinder its spread. Repentance should come at the point of guilt the Holy Spirit is revealing at the moment, such as crucifying Jesus in this particular case. It would be unwise to include that point in a message to Jews today, and irrelevant in a message to Gentiles. Anointed preaching will reveal the points at which the Holy Spirit Himself is doing the convicting, and this brings positive response.

The technical term for this initial step of repentance and faith in Jesus Christ is "discipling." The subsequent lifetime road of discipleship, beginning then and producing the ethical changes that mold disciples into Christlikeness, is called "perfecting." As missiologist Donald McGavran says, "Antigrowth concepts arise from confusing perfecting with discipling."[8] Peter did not make that mistake.

Baptism. Baptism is the primary outward, visible action that validates the inward decision to follow Jesus Christ as Lord and Savior. For most segments of Christianity, baptism is the principal initiatory rite that identifies believers with the Body of

Christ, the Church. Peter did not suggest postponing baptism until a certain stage of perfection had been reached. His word was that if they were serious about receiving remission of their sins, they should prove it by being baptized immediately.

The Results of a Great Day for God's Kingdom

41. Then those who gladly received his word were baptized; and that day about three thousand souls were added to them.

The results of Pentecost included both *quantitative* church growth and *qualitative* church growth. The two should never be thought of as separate. Healthy churches usually grow. Unhealthy churches tend not to grow.

Putting together a scenario in which 3,000 were baptized in one day, beginning around noon, is an interesting challenge. If only the 12 were doing the baptizing, it would mean 42 an hour for each of the apostles. It could be done. I recently received a newspaper report from South Africa describing a baptism of 70,000 in one day performed by 1 archbishop and 21 bishops. This would have been 23.3 times the number baptized on Pentecost. The quantitative growth begun at Pentecost is not only continuing today, but it is also increasing.

Of all the descriptions of Christian churches in the New Testament, this first church planted in Jerusalem on the Day of Pentecost is the one a great many today would choose to imitate if they could. It was not only a megachurch, but it was also of high quality.

42. And they continued steadfastly in the apostles' doctrine

and fellowship, in the breaking of bread, and in prayers.
43. Then fear came upon every soul, and many wonders
and signs were done through the apostles. 44. Now all
who believed were together, and had all things in
common, 45. and sold their possessions and goods, and
divided them among all, as anyone had need. 46. So
continuing daily with one accord in the temple,
and breaking bread from house to house, they ate
their food with gladness and simplicity of heart,
47. praising God and having favor with all the people....

Luke records six distinct areas reflecting the spiritual quality of this young church. The leadership of the apostles was undoubtedly a major contributing factor to new converts maturing in Christ so rapidly. Another factor would have been the relatively low threshold for devout Jews to decide to cross over and follow Jesus as their Messiah. They still worshiped on the Sabbath in the Temple, they kept the law and they maintained their existing social and family ties. The threshold would be much higher for Gentiles later on in Acts.

The Six Spiritual Qualities

Learning more about God. The phrase **apostles' doctrine** means teaching in general, not just theology per se. The believers submitted to the spiritual authority of the apostles and followed their leadership. Because the apostles had just received 40 days of Jesus' teaching **things pertaining to the kingdom of God** (1:3), it is easy to imagine that much of what the apostles taught through deed and word would have been this. The Jews' belief in Jehovah God was solid, but the new believers had to adjust to being **in the last days** (2:17) according to the fulfillment of Joel's prophecy, particularly to move daily in the power of the Holy Spirit which had never previously been possible for the Jewish rank and file.

Fellowship with one another. While they were growing in their vertical relationship to God, the new believers were also growing in their horizontal relationship to each other in Christian fellowship. This relationship is stressed heavily here, mentioned in four of the six verses in the passage. One of the key factors of church health is to design ways and means for fellowship to be an integral part of church life week in and week out. If it is absent, the church will tend to plateau or decline. New members must be absorbed fairly rapidly. This is one of the reasons the cell church movement is having an increasing impact, not only in Korea where it is most highly developed, but also in many other parts of the world.

In Jerusalem, eating together was important. Many scholars feel that **the breaking of bread** in 2:42 can mean the Lord's Supper, but that **breaking bread from house to house** in 2:46 means sharing meals with other believers at home. Both are important in building strong foundations for a growing church.

These believers were also more radical in their giving to the church and sharing material possessions than many of us are today. Their relationships with each other were so strong that they could not tolerate anyone in the church living with material need while others enjoyed relative prosperity. As family members will frequently do for each other, they **sold their possessions and goods** so they would have resources to care for the needy. They apparently were going far beyond the tithe, which they would have done in any case as part of their Jewish law.

Churches in which members do not at least tithe their income, that is, give at least 10 percent to the Lord's work and primarily to the local church, are obviously not high-quality churches. Jesus taught that this is an important outward sign of inward commitment to God when He said, "For where your treasure is, there your heart will be also" (Luke 12:34). Pastors who desire to measure the commitment of their members should begin by looking at their giving records. In Jerusalem, the believers would not have been embarrassed by this, as would the members of many of today's churches.

Worshiping God. The believers customarily went to the Temple daily, and there they would worship God and thank Him for sending His Messiah. Worship in our day is becoming a more and more high profile activity in many churches than it has been in past generations.

In fact, a worldwide phenomenon seems to be emerging around a relatively new form of worship. It could well be that the most powerful unifying factor among the postdenominational churches, exploding in growth on every continent, is long periods of praise and worship based on contemporary spiritual songs composed month after month by members of the local congregation or of the particular apostolic network in which it participates. This style of worship allows great latitude for body language, and is typically peppered with enthusiastic applause directed toward God Himself. Increasing numbers of more traditional churches are now moving from pipe organs, pianos and choirs toward contemporary worship.

Prayer. Prayer, presumably both corporate and individual, characterized the Jerusalem church. This has been a severely neglected area of our Christian life in many of our churches today. Prayer is ordinarily talked about much and practiced little. But things are changing. Since about 1970, a great worldwide prayer movement has been sweeping across churches, more strongly in some areas than others. Previous to 1970, the churches of all denominations in Korea had been setting an example for the world. They have been accustomed to practicing prayer as much as talking about it, and the quantitative and qualitative growth of Korean churches has led the whole world over the past decades. Korean pastors are the first to stress prayer in both deed and word. Early morning prayer meetings year around, all night prayer on Friday nights and fasting and prayer retreats on multiple prayer mountains are as characteristic of Korean churches as preaching sermons or taking up offerings.

Power ministries. When we read that **fear came upon every soul**, the meaning is not that the believers were scared of something, but that they were in awe of the power of God that was constantly manifesting around them. The apostles were modeling the continuance of the signs and wonders characteristic of the days when they were with Jesus. Healings and deliverances from demons would be commonplace in the life of the Jerusalem church, just as they are in many churches today. For example, in Argentina, where a notable revival is now in progress, most churches practice power ministries as they did in Jerusalem. In fact, one of the churches in Buenos Aires has a staff member who has the title "minister of miracles," and part of the job description is to collect the medical and legal evidence necessary to verify some of the unusual miracles such as teeth being filled, obese people instantly losing weight and new hair growth on bald heads. When things such as this happen, naturally, both believers and unbelievers are in awe before the amazing power of God.

Outreach. Reaching the lost was a priority for this church from the beginning. They had **favor with all the people**, meaning those who had not yet accepted Jesus as their Messiah and been baptized into the Church. Such fellowship, worship and miraculous power of God would have made it easy for the believers to turn inward, to say that we need to learn more about Jesus and to relate more intimately with Him, neglecting the lost people out

there in their community. But they did not yield to this temptation, as we know from the concluding sentence of Acts 2:

**47. ...And the Lord added to the church daily those
who were being saved.**

What a church!

Reflection Questions

1. Review and discuss the three visible signs of the invisible
   Spirit: audible, visual and oral. Have you ever heard of or
   experienced personally anything like that today?
2. This chapter contends that Pentecost was a truly *cross-cultural* missionary incident even though Jews were preaching to
   Jews. How do you explain this?
3. Do you think that every Christian should speak in tongues at
   some time or other? How does your answer relate to the "gift
   of tongues"?
4. Name the three phases of the "Pentecost event" and relate
   each one to breaking a missiological barrier.
5. The church that started in Jerusalem at Pentecost was in
   many ways an ideal church. What were some of its characteristics that our churches today would do well to imitate?

Notes
1. Donald A. McGavran, *Understanding Church Growth* (Grand Rapids, MI:
   William B. Eerdmans Publishing Co., Third Edition, 1990), p. 26. Used by
   permission.
2. Ibid., p. 30.

3. Reprinted from *Jerusalem in the Time of Jesus* by Joachim Jeremias, copyright © 1969 SCM. Used by permission of Augsburg Fortress (p. 84).
4. C. Peter Wagner, *Your Spiritual Gifts Can Help Your Church Grow* (Ventura, CA: Regal Books, 1994), p. 204.
5. Simon J. Kistemaker, *New Testament Commentary: Exposition on the Acts of the Apostles* (Grand Rapids, MI: Baker Book House Company, 1990), p. 78. Used by permission.
6. Stanley M. Horton, *The Book of Acts* (Springfield, MO: Gospel Publishing House, 1981), p. 106.
7. Hermann Haarbeck, "Word, Tongue, Utterance," *The New International Dictionary of New Testament Theology*, Colin Brown, ed. (Grand Rapids, MI: Zondervan Publishing House, 1971, 1978), Vol. 3, p. 1080.
8. McGavran, *Understanding Church Growth*, p. 123.

One Hundred Thirty Converts a Day Can Shake a City

Acts 3 and 4

Once the Day of Pentecost and the Feast of Harvest had ended, and the tens of thousands of pilgrims who had come to Jerusalem for the festival had gone home, the city almost returned to normal. But not quite. Things would never be the same, as we see from Peter and John's rather casual and routine visit to the Temple about three months later.

A Miracle in Plain Sight
Acts 3

1. Now Peter and John went up together to the temple at the hour of prayer, the ninth hour.
2. And a certain man lame from his mother's womb was carried, whom they laid daily at the gate of the temple

> which is called Beautiful, to ask alms from those who
> entered the temple; 3. who, seeing Peter and John
> about to go into the temple, asked for alms.

Peter and John had grown up together in the fishing community of Bethsaida in Galilee. Along with James, they had been given the privilege of forming the inner circle of three who were personally the closest to Jesus. They were the only ones who had been eyewitnesses of Jesus' transfiguration (see Matt. 17:1), and they were the three whom Jesus called apart from the other eight when He went to His prayer vigil in Gethsemane (see Mark 14:33).

Messianic Jews

For Peter and John and the other disciples, going to the Temple at three in the afternoon for the daily prayer meeting was routine. When they could, they also, undoubtedly, attended the other two daily prayer meetings that were held mornings and evenings. We sometimes forget that, at this point in time, none of the believers was a "Christian" in the proper sense of the word. They were known as "disciples of Jesus the Messiah," or as "the brethren," or as "followers of The Way," or as "believers," but they were Jews. Believers were not called "Christians" until almost 15 years later when Gentile churches began to be planted in Antioch.

Those who participate in the growing Messianic Jewish movement today prefer to be called "Messianic Jews" rather than "Christians." They remind us that, whereas, in biblical times many Jewish followers of Jesus had to be reprimanded for attempting to "Judaize" the Gentiles and, thereby, block them from accepting Christ, so today many Gentile believers insist on

"Gentilizing" the Jews, and they should likewise be reprimanded. Both of these errors violate the principle of contextualization I have mentioned previously, and they prevent the gospel from effectively being carried across cultural barriers. They throw accepting Christ into a *cultural* mode rather than allowing it to become an essentially *religious* decision, and predictably retard world evangelization.

Peter and John, as well as all the other disciples of the day, looked like Jews, talked like Jews, behaved like Jews, regarded themselves as Jews and were seen by the unbelievers as Jews, although perhaps of a rather odd variety. As a missiologist, unlike many previous commentators, I am personally so sensitized to this that I find myself having a hard time using the term "Christian" to refer to the believers until we come to Acts 11:26, where we read, **And the disciples were first called Christians in Antioch.** Peter, the apostle to the circumcision (Jews), much later accepted the term, but I would imagine quite reluctantly. He writes, "Yet if anyone suffers as a Christian" (1 Pet. 4:16). Actually, other than these two appearances, the word "Christian" is used only once more in the Bible, where Agrippa, a Gentile, says to Paul, the apostle to the Gentiles, **"You almost persuade me to become a Christian"** (Acts 26:28).

The Lame Beggar

Those who are familiar with societies that have a strong presence of beggars take them for granted. Beggars are a familiar daily sight in cities. They attract no more special attention than do people who might be buying a hot dog or a crowd waiting for a theater to open or passengers getting off a bus. They are part of the way life is and, as far as the average citizens are concerned, the way it always has been.

Furthermore, individual beggars, particularly the immobile ones, have personal jurisdiction over a physical turf they have staked out, usually on a busy sidewalk. They are in the same place every day, seven days a week. In some Latin American cities they have gone as far as to organize beggars' unions. My friend Sam Wilson once told me that one time when he was in Cuzco, Peru, the beggars went out on strike until the merchants agreed to double their daily handouts!

When Doris and I were raising our family in Cochabamba, Bolivia, we would always have the children give some money to the "shaky man" who was on the sidewalk near the door to our church. If he wasn't there some Sunday, we would assume he must be sick and we would be concerned about him even though he couldn't talk and we never knew his name. Many of these beggars make a reasonable living, although they would not appear so by their dress and lifestyle. From time to time, however, newspapers report stories about beggars who have died and left considerable sums of money behind in their quarters.

This, I think, could fairly well describe the scenario that faced Peter and John as they went into the Temple. They must have seen that same lame man a hundred times and may well have occasionally dropped coins into his tin cup. In fact, Jesus, who also was a Jew and frequented the Temple while in Jerusalem, must have passed him many times as well. Everyone, including Peter, John, Jesus and hundreds who saw him every day, knew he couldn't walk, due to a birth defect, and had to be carried by others to his place. If his picture had appeared in a newspaper, a large percentage of Jerusalem residents would have said, "Oh, yes, I recognize that man. He sits at the Beautiful Gate."

It was a perfect setup for a public miracle to be done in plain sight.

Instant Healing

....

4. And fixing his eyes on him, with John, Peter said,
"Look at us." 5. So he gave them his attention,
expecting to receive something from them. 6. Then Peter
said, "Silver and gold I do not have, but what I do have
I give you: In the name of Jesus Christ of Nazareth,
rise up and walk." 7. And he took him by the right
hand and lifted him up, and immediately his feet
and ankle bones received strength.

....

Saying to a beggar, "look at us," was out of the ordinary. Part of the expected behavior pattern in a beggar society is not to make eye contact. The beggar would have instantly understood that Peter was establishing a social relationship, brief as it might have been. Because the beggar was asking for alms, he undoubtedly expected a handout. Peter's statement that they had no money would have been both unexpected and unwelcome, because receiving money was the highest agenda item on the beggar's mind at the time. Peter's words did not imply that the disciples were poverty-stricken, but more likely that they were not carrying any money with them at the time. But he was about to offer the beggar something money couldn't buy.

I would surmise that because the beggar was lame from birth, the possibility that he would ever walk had never entered his mind, anymore than a person born with blue eyes would ever expect them to turn brown. Peter didn't find it necessary to stop to interview the man or to prepare him emotionally for what was about to happen. He spoke to the man in Jesus' name and commanded him to **rise up and walk**. The man was instantly healed in plain sight of everyone else walking into the Temple that afternoon!

This was not the first miracle done by the apostles after Jesus' ascension. We have already seen that **many wonders and signs were done through the apostles** (Acts 2:43). But other than the miracle of languages on the Day of Pentecost, this is the first one described in detail. Because this is all part of Luke's way of preparing the kickoff for at least 2,000 years of subsequent world evangelization, such an initial mighty work of God needs some analysis. Luke highlights at least four important points here.

The Medical Report

Luke, a physician, gives details—such as the bones of the feet and ankles receiving strength, Peter grasping him by the *right* hand, and the fact that it was a birth defect—other reporters without medical training might not have mentioned. Furthermore, long, drawn-out physical therapy did not seem to be needed, as it is after much orthopedic surgery today. In moments, the invalid was leaping and running around. He didn't even have to teach himself to walk, which is surprising, given the fact that he had never previously learned how. This healing could only be regarded as being caused by miraculous supernatural power, not explained away as an obvious wrong medical diagnosis, the only respectable explanation some physicians choose to give for similar miracles today.

Luke, of course, was not a personal eyewitness of this event. Yet, he reports it as a straightforward fact. The issue of how miracles are verified and how the true is distinguished from the false is an important one, which I will deal with again when we later come to some other dramatic events, such as raising the dead. But meanwhile, at least for Luke, who was a physician, the secondhand accounts of credible witnesses apparently were sufficient evidence for him to report the miracle in some detail to his friend Theophilus. In all probability, no physician at all was involved with the incident, and, therefore, medical reports were not available to consult. If Peter and John said it happened, that would have been enough for Luke.

The Authority to Heal

Peter was no novice at divine healing. He had healed many, both before and after the resurrection of Jesus. We can assume, therefore, that he chose his words carefully when he said, **"What I do have I give you."**

What is it that Peter had, and where did he get it?

First of all, we must observe that Peter apparently had something in his personal possession that he could use at will, parallel to money, which he didn't have at the moment but which he could have spent as he desired. The thing that Peter had, and could give away, was healing power. It had been included in Jesus' promise that **you shall receive power when the Holy Spirit has come upon you** (Acts 1:8). Jesus had told Peter and the others that they could expect to do the works He did, explaining that the power of the Holy Spirit they would receive was the same power by which He did His healing miracles.

Later, Paul explains that "gifts of healings" are given by the Holy Spirit to some members of the Body of Christ (see 1 Cor. 12:9), in the same way that others have spiritual gifts of teaching or administration or helps or prophecy. Would Peter have been given a gift of healing? I believe he probably had the gift, knowing a good deal about Peter's subsequent career. But for a healing such as the lame man at the Temple gate, a gift of healing is not always a necessary prerequisite. For example, all Christians have a *role* of witnessing for Jesus, even if they do not have the *gift* of evangelist. I believe that all Christians have a *role* of praying for the sick. Even by using a role, the healing could have taken place.

Those who do have the gift of healing fully realize that the power to heal is not innate in them, except to the extent that the Holy Spirit dwells within them. That is why Peter, using a frequent pattern for healing ministries, said, **"In the name of Jesus Christ of Nazareth."** This was a statement of authority, again not intrinsic authority, but authority delegated to him by Jesus.

When Jesus first sent Peter and the others out to heal the sick, He gave them power to do it (see Matt. 10:1). The Greek word for this power is *exousia,* which carries with it the meaning that the power is not inherent but delegated by a higher authority. It is similar to the power an ambassador has been given by the president. U.S. ambassadors, for example, would get nowhere in foreign countries by presenting themselves in their own names. Rather, they say, "I come in the name of the President of the United States." That is exactly why Peter said he had come, **"In the name of Jesus Christ of Nazareth."**

Some may observe that in Acts 1:8, when Jesus says, **"You shall receive power,"** He uses another common Greek word, *dunamis.* This word does imply "strength based on inherent physical, spiritual, or natural powers" according to *The New International Dictionary of New Testament Theology.*[1] It implies that the disciples from then on would have the indwelling *dunamis* power of the Holy Spirit, but that their spiritual power could only be used by the *authority* given by Jesus. Invoking the name of Jesus is a declaration of the authority to heal.

Faith in Healing

It is obvious that the faith of this beggar, either in Jesus Christ or in divine healing, had nothing to do with the miracle. As I have read other commentaries on this passage, I have been surprised that this seems to bother some. Without mentioning names, I will say that one excellent commentator affirms that in the New Testament, miracles are connected with faith, with which I agree. But from that he deduces that this crippled man could only walk if he had put his faith in Jesus. Another says that we can *assume* he became a believer. I don't think either one of these will satisfy closer scrutiny.

The New Testament has examples of three different possible agents of the faith necessary for divine healing to take place, the sick person being only one of the possible agents.

When two blind men came to Jesus (see Matt. 9:27-31), He said, "Do you believe that I am able to do this?" When they affirmed that they did, Jesus said, "According to your faith let it be to you" (v. 29). They were both healed, and their personal faith played an important role. The sick person in that case was the agent of faith for healing. But this is not the only way it happens.

Another agent of faith is an intermediary. A Roman centurion once asked Jesus for healing on behalf of his servant who was paralyzed, perhaps much like the lame man at the Temple gate. In this case, Jesus congratulated the centurion and said, "I have not found such great *faith*, not even in Israel!" (Matt. 8:10). Not only did the servant have no faith, but he probably had no idea who Jesus was or that his master was asking for healing. Nevertheless, he was miraculously healed through the faith of an intermediary.

The third agent of faith is the person who does the healing. Unless we read things into the text that are not here, the most reasonable conclusion is that the agents of faith for the healing of the lame beggar were Peter and John.

We might hope that the beggar was saved, but if he wasn't, he would not be the first to experience miraculous healing without a subsequent commitment to Christian discipleship. John 6, for example, begins with many people following Jesus "because they saw His signs which He performed on those who were diseased" (John 6:2). But before the chapter ends, Jesus has to say, "There are some of you who do not believe" (John 6:64). And, "From that time many of His disciples went back and walked with Him no more" (John 6:66). The fact that the beggar "praised God" proves no more than that he was doing what all Jews are supposed to do when they go into the Temple, and that he acknowledged his healing came from Jehovah.

As I have pointed out previously, healing by itself does not save. Healing can open people's minds to consider the gospel, but only a response to the gospel and personal faith in Jesus Christ as Savior and Lord can save.

The Timing

If Jesus Himself had passed this lame man when going in and out of the Temple, and if Peter and John had seen him there day after day, why had no one healed him previously?

A key to ministering with divine healing is to be sensitive to God's timing. Jesus said, "The Son can do nothing of Himself, but what He sees the Father do" (John 5:19). Jesus' miraculous works were done according to the Father's timing. Peter was obviously following this lead. On this particular trip to the Temple, Peter had extraordinary compassion on the lame man and a great desire to see him healed. Where did this desire come from? Presumably from the Father, "For it is God who works in you both to will and to do for His good pleasure" (Phil. 2:13). Why the Father chose this particular time, and not another, we may never know.

Because Peter was so sure of the timing of the Father, he chose not to pray a prayer of intercession, asking God to heal the lame man, which is the most common form of healing prayer. He spoke directly to the lame man and commanded him to stand up!

An Exuberant Testimony

8. So he, leaping up, stood and walked and entered the
temple with them—walking, leaping, and praising God.
9. And all the people saw him walking and praising God.
11. Now as the lame man who was healed held on to
Peter and John, all the people ran together to them in
the porch which is called Solomon's, greatly amazed.

The healed man let everybody know he was healed. An impossible dream had come true! He testified by deed: walking and jumping! He testified by word: praising God! He recognized that it was God who had healed him. Peter did not seek or receive any credit. He didn't pass the offering plate and take a collection for his ministry. The focus and the glory was on God.

The people in the Temple who saw it could neither ignore nor doubt the power behind Peter's use of the name of Jesus Christ of Nazareth. They all had known this lame man and now they saw him whole. They were as surprised and amazed as the others had been three months earlier when they heard the tongues spoken on the Day of Pentecost. And they were just as ready as the others to listen to Peter's explanation.

Peter's Interpretation of the Miracle

12. So when Peter saw it, he responded to the people:
"Men of Israel, why do you marvel at this? Or
why look so intently at us, as though by our
own power or godliness we had made this man walk?
13. The God of Abraham, Isaac, and Jacob, the
God of our fathers, glorified His Servant Jesus,...

**16. And His name, through faith in His name,
has made this man strong, whom you see and know. Yes,
the faith which comes through Him has given him this
perfect soundness in the presence of you all.**

As he addressed this second group in the Temple, Peter took wise precautions to assure them he was still a bona fide Jew. Phrases such as "men of Israel"; "the God of Abraham, Isaac and Jacob"; "the God of our fathers" knit him with the audience and helped them ignore the fact that he was speaking with an unsophisticated Galilean accent. His biblical text was from Moses, and he mentioned Samuel and the prophets. What had been happening over the past three months was the introduction to a new era in the total history of salvation, nothing less than a new covenant. But as a good communicator, Peter began with the old covenant, which was known, and then moved to the new covenant, which, for the Jews, was as yet unknown.

However, they liked what they heard about this new covenant very much because Peter helped them understand the true power behind the miracle. He explains that it was not some power inherent in Peter or John, and Peter appropriately uses the word *dunamis* here (v. 12). Peter does not mention the power of the Holy Spirit at this point because it only would have confused them. Some of them would have heard Peter say, "In the name of Jesus Christ of Nazareth," and they knew who Jesus was well enough to cringe when Peter reminded them, as he also did on Pentecost, that they were corporately guilty of crucifying the true Servant of God. He told them that Jesus had been raised from the dead, and that they should receive and respect Him now if they had not done so previously.

Many of them wanted to get in touch with the power of Jesus

that they had seen with their own eyes. Peter, therefore, took the opportunity to make three demands:

1. Repent

> **19. Repent therefore and be converted,... 26. ...in turning away every one of you from your iniquities.**

This is the same thing Peter said on the Day of Pentecost. They had to repent of killing the Messiah even though they may have been ignorant of what they were doing at the time (see 3:17). Ignorance of sin does not excuse it and erase guilt, particularly when the sin has done damage to others. It needs to be confessed.

Identificational Repentance

Acts 3:19 is one of the principal places in the New Testament where we run across the concept of identificational repentance. Identificational repentance means confessing and remitting sins we may not have committed personally, but with which we are identified for one reason or another. It is what Daniel did when he said he was "speaking, praying, and confessing my sin and *the sin of my people Israel*" (Dan. 9:20), and what Nehemiah meant when he confessed to God, "Both *my father's house* and I have sinned" (Neh. 1:6).

Obviously, very few of the Jews here at the Temple, or among the Hellenists who were visiting Jerusalem on the Day of Pentecost, would personally have been in the crowd who shouted to Pilate, "Crucify Him, crucify Him!" (Luke 23:21). None of them would have been among the Roman authorities who actually passed the sentence or among the soldiers who nailed Him to the cross. Nevertheless, Peter demanded that they repent of crucifying Jesus, and many of them did.

As we advance in our knowledge of strategic-level spiritual warfare, the principles and practice of identificational repentance are assuming more and more of a central role. Books by John Dawson, such as *Taking Our Cities for God* (Creation House) and *Healing America's Wounds* (Regal Books) and by Cindy Jacobs, such as *Possessing the Gates of the Enemy* (Chosen Books), have been helpful in understanding how to do identificational repentance. I have also written about it in *Warfare Prayer* (Regal Books), my book on strategic-level spiritual warfare.

2. Receive Forgiveness

> 19. ...that your sins may be blotted out, so that times of refreshing may come from the presence of the Lord.

Repenting and placing faith in Jesus Christ will allow God not only to forgive sins, but also to *obliterate* them. We ourselves may remember them later, but God refuses to. Peter was saying that God would not only forgive the people for crucifying Jesus, but that all the rest of their sins would be forgiven as well. They could hardly have comprehended fully that this would mean, for example, that there would be no more need to observe an annual day of atonement, but they could at least begin to understand it somewhat. The more they understood it, the more spiritual *refreshing* they would experience. Many of them received this as "good news," another term for the gospel.

3. Join Forces for World Evangelization

> 25. You are the sons of the prophets, and of the covenant which God made with our fathers, saying to Abraham, "And in your seed all the families of the earth shall be blessed."

This quote from Genesis 12:3 is the Great Commission in its Old Testament version. The "families" of the earth is a synonym for "nations" or "peoples" from the Greek word *ethnos*, the word Jesus used when He commanded His followers to "make disciples of all the *nations*" (Matt. 28:19). This was such a radical suggestion to the ethnic Jews (mostly Hebrews in this case) whom Peter was addressing, that I would imagine very few, if any, would have picked up the significance of Peter's challenge. But Peter would not have forgotten that God gave him and the others the power of the Holy Spirit, not just to heal lame beggars, but also to be effective witnesses in Jerusalem, Judea, Samaria and the end of the earth.

Going to Jail for Doing Good
Acts 4

1. Now as they spoke to the people, the priests, the captain of the temple, and the Sadducees came upon them, 2. being greatly disturbed that they taught the people and preached in Jesus the resurrection from the dead. 3. And they laid hands on them, and put them in custody until the next day, for it was already evening.

The word about what was happening in a certain section of the Temple grounds that afternoon spread throughout the rest of the Temple. The beggar was healed before 3:00 P.M., but the Temple officers didn't show up until later, when the gates of the Temple were to have been closed. By then, it must have been clear that this unexpected event could be escalating to the point where it could threaten Jerusalem's status quo. In any case, it had upset the peace and quiet of the daily Temple routine and rituals. So a group of authorities decided to put a stop to it.

Some **priests** who happened to be on duty in the Temple at the time came with the others. Priests and Levites administered the daily sacrifices.

The captain of the temple was the chief of the Temple police. He was second in command to the high priest himself, and his presence signaled that the disturbance, as they regarded it, was being taken very seriously by Temple leaders. He undoubtedly had several Temple police officers with him.

The appearance of the **Sadducees** has more than a passing significance. They were not a large group in Jerusalem, but they had gained disproportionate political power. The Romans largely left the internal affairs of Jerusalem in the hands of a Jewish aristocracy, and as Richard Rackham says, "This hierarchical aristocracy was Sadducean in theology. In fact the high priest and they that were with him practically formed the sect of the Sadducees."[2]

The Sadducees did not pay much attention to Jesus in the early part of His ministry, but toward the end, when it became evident that political implications may be involved, they actively opposed Him. Why? They were part of the Jewish aristocracy and, as Donald Hagner points out, were, therefore, very much interested in maintaining the status quo. "It follows," says Hagner, "that they pursued policies designed to appease the governing authorities of Rome."[3] Thus, for a political reason they did not like the looks of the disturbance in the Temple.

Underlying spiritual reasons were present as well. Peter had openly proclaimed **in Jesus the resurrection from the dead,** but the Sadducees believed "that there is no resurrection of the dead, nor any future life whether of bliss or sorrow."[4] For this reason the Pharisees, who included such biblical notables as Nicodemus, Gamaliel and Saul of Tarsus, seem to be less opposed than the Sadducees to Jesus' movement as it develops under the apostles. In fact, Rackham suggests that many of the Pharisees "were secretly delighted to have the aid of the new teachers in vigorously asserting the doctrine of the resurrection as against the Sadducees."[5]

The Pharisees, along with the apostles of Jesus, had a further problem with the Sadducees who, as Hagner says, "appear to have rejected the belief in angels and demons."[6] No wonder Jesus said to the Sadducees in disgust, "You do not know the Scriptures nor the power of God" (Mark 12:24). Not knowing the power of God would make it very difficult, if not impossible, for the Sadducees to gain any realistic understanding of the explosive spread of the gospel with the miraculous events accompanying it both up to then and even more so in the future.

A Church Growth Report

----

4. However, many of those who heard the word believed; and the number of the men came to be about five thousand.

No particular literary reason exists for this statement to be inserted into a narrative that begins with the arrest of the apostles and continues in the very next verse with the trial before the Sanhedrin the following morning. Why, then, is it here? Apparently, Luke wants to remind us what the ultimate objective of activities, such as healing lame people, preaching to crowds in the temple, and suffering persecution, continues to be, namely, making disciples of all nations including Jerusalem, Judea, Samaria and the end of the earth.

The part where the apostles are put into jail for doing the good deed of healing a lame man could be discouraging for the readers. So Luke, as he does from time to time, pauses ever so briefly to give us a progress report on the spread of the gospel. It seems that Luke was quite pragmatic, in the good sense of the word. He clearly understood what the goals were and measured success or failure against the goals. Ernst Haenchen says, "Luke loves the multitudes of converts, the mass-successes. Not that he was unduly impressed by sheer numbers. But the crowds streaming into the fold of Christ are for him the visible expression of the divine blessing resting on the Church."[7]

The number "5,000" is impressive, purposely so if Luke inserted this report in order to encourage believers in the midst of an account of persecution. If the 5,000 consisted of the believers in Jerusalem, the Church would have grown from 3,000 on Pentecost to 5,000 three months later, or by 20 converts a day. However, the calculations appear to be somewhat more complex than that.

For one thing, if the picture we have of the crowd at Pentecost is correct, many of the 3,000 converts on that day would have been Hellenistic Jews who had come as pilgrims to the Feast of Harvest in Jerusalem, but then returned to any number of other cities and provinces. The fact that the gospel was preached in at least 16 languages that day causes us to suppose that they had scattered back to at least 16 language areas, probably many more. How many of the 3,000 were Hebrews who would have stayed in Jerusalem or other parts of Palestine and how many were visiting Hellenists we are not told.

In any case, the 3,000 on Pentecost is probably not a figure exclusively for believers with permanent residence in Jerusalem. Perhaps the 5,000 should not be taken as such a figure either. It could mean Jerusalem only, it could mean the city and the surrounding countryside in Judea, or it could mean the number of Messianic Jews wherever they might live.

Whatever the scope, the total of believers would be more than 5,000 because the 5,000 are men only. Here the Greek word *aner*, meaning men as opposed to women, rather than the Greek *anthropos*, which includes both men and women, is used.

Men would be regarded as heads of households, and the ordinary pattern of conversion in that culture would have been that when the head of the household makes a decision of such a magnitude, it is a decision for the rest of the family as well. A conservative estimate of one woman and one child for each man would put the figure at 15,000 believers. It could be considerably higher because many Jewish households would have included more than just the nuclear family, and also parents having just one child was not the ordinary pattern.

If the number of believers were 15,000 or more, the figure would then be disproportionate to Joachim Jeremias's estimate of 25,000 or 30,000, mentioned in the last chapter, as the total population of Jerusalem. One explanation of this is that Jeremias's figure may be too low. Howard Marshall says, "Estimates of the total population of Jerusalem range from 25,000 to about ten times that figure."[8] The probability is that, in the absence of Bureaus of the Census, no one really knows and, therefore, no one can pinpoint the exact scope of Luke's figure.

Whether it was for Jerusalem specifically or for the believing community in general, the church growth from 3,000 to 15,000 in three months calculates to 130 new converts a day. This kind of momentum, which at least would have included the city of Jerusalem, would be enough to concern the Sadducees and other groups in power. It would also cause them to act as decisively as they could when a public incident, such as the healing of the lame man in the Temple, would provide a plausible excuse.

Explaining Spiritual Power to the Establishment

5. And it came to pass, on the next day, that their rulers, elders, and scribes, 6. as well as Annas the high priest,

> Caiaphas, John, and Alexander, and as many as were of the
> family of the high priest, were gathered together at Jerusalem.

Although he doesn't use the word as such, Luke here describes a
meeting of the Sanhedrin, referred to as **the council** later in verse
15. This was no insignificant group. F. F. Bruce says the
Sanhedrin was "the senate and supreme court of the Jewish
nation."[9] The situation must have been considered extremely
serious for such an array of dignitaries to make room on their cal-
endars for this impromptu meeting.

The Sanhedrin consisted of 70 members plus the high priest,
who served as president. Bruce says, "The Sanhedrin at this time
included a majority of members from the Sadducean party, sup-
porting the chief-priestly interests, and a powerful minority from
the Pharisaic party, to whom most of the scribes or professional
exponents of the Law belonged."[10] They are referred to here as
rulers, elders, and scribes. They were basically in charge of the
affairs of the Jewish nation, so Peter and John had been taken
right to the top.

> **7. And when they had set them in the midst, they asked,**
> **"By what power or by what name have you done this?"**

These people, who were sitting as judges over Peter and John,
were the same ones who, only a few months earlier, had met for
the trial of Jesus, and then they must have felt that they had put
a stop to any potential uprising by having the Roman government crucify Him. But now the *name* of Jesus surfaces in a dramatic way once again, and they are visibly concerned. Killing
Jesus, apparently, hadn't stopped the movement! When they ask
"by what name," they are clearly raising the question of author-

ity, as I have mentioned previously. They are anxious to protect their own authority, and predictably nervous about anyone who had claimed to be King of the Jews. They must have known that by then perhaps 10 percent or 20 percent of their city was following Jesus, or at least were favorable toward the movement.

It is significant that they do not raise the question of the validity of the miracle, as such tribunals might do in today's rationalistic and scientific age. They shared basic worldviews with the apostles, and therefore, were not disposed to question the supernatural power that seemed to dwell in Peter and John. Their question was much more insidious. Simon Kistemaker says that by emphasizing the pronoun *you*, "The apostles are addressed as if they, with the beggar as their accomplice, have perpetrated a crime."[11]

But the Sanhedrin's question, as we well know, was a setup for Peter's chance to testify to them about the power of Jesus. Peter remembered well that Jesus had said, "They will lay their hands on you and persecute you,...and you will be brought before kings and rulers for My name's sake. But it will turn out for you as an occasion for testimony" (Luke 21:12,13).

> 8. Then Peter, filled with the Holy Spirit, said to them, "Rulers of the people and elders of Israel:
> 9. If we this day are judged for a good deed done to the helpless man, by what means he has been made well, 10. let it be known to you all, and to all the people of Israel, that by the name of Jesus Christ of Nazareth, whom you crucified, whom God raised from the dead, by Him this man stands before you whole."

Although it was not true of everything Peter ever did or said, on this occasion, as on the Day of Pentecost, he was filled with the Holy Spirit. This is not a mere reiteration of the theological fact that all true Christian believers are indwelt by the Holy Spirit. At conversion, we are all "made to drink into one Spirit" (1 Cor. 12:13). Paul also says, "The Spirit of Him who raised Jesus from the dead dwells in you" (Rom. 8:11). Being "filled with the Spirit" is a special empowering of the Holy Spirit over and above the ordinary, but something that God desires and that we as individuals are actively to pursue. I make a habit daily of asking God to fill me with His Holy Spirit, and I believe He does, because Jesus said that just as a good father will not give a scorpion to a son who asks for an egg, "How much more will your heavenly Father give the Holy Spirit to those who ask Him!" (Luke 11:13).

Under a special anointing of the Holy Spirit, Peter answers the Sanhedrin both defensively and offensively.

By way of defense, Peter explains how the miracle happened. He affirms what the Sadducees in the room did not want to hear, namely, that the man they had crucified had been raised from the dead, and that it was by His power and through the authority of His name that the beggar was healed.

Peter could have elaborated a bit and stopped there. He had answered their question. But the Holy Spirit, who had filled Peter, moved him forward to turn the tables. They had implied that Peter was guilty of a crime, but now Peter becomes the accuser: "You crucified Him!" They had sinned against God because (1) God had raised Jesus from the dead to prove His authenticity, and (2) Jewish Scripture had predicted it in Psalms 118:22: "The stone which the builders rejected has become the chief cornerstone." Peter then sums it up by saying:

....

12. Nor is there salvation in any other, for there is no

> other name under heaven given among men
> by which we must be saved.

Few, if any, of the priests or leaders responded positively and accepted Jesus as their Messiah at this stage. Later on many of them did, but at this time they still hadn't come to terms with the fact that Jesus' kingdom was not of this world, and their personal and most immediate desire was to protect the political status quo in Jerusalem.

A Threat with No Substance

> 15. But when they had commanded them to go aside out of the council, they conferred among themselves, 16. saying, "What shall we do to these men? For, indeed, that a notable miracle has been done through them is evident to all who dwell in Jerusalem, and we cannot deny it. 17. But so that it spreads no further among the people, let us severely threaten them, that from now on they speak to no man in this name."

The members of the Sanhedrin were astonished at hearing such things from these Galileans whom they considered **uneducated and untrained** (4:13). If taken literally, the word for "uneducated," *agrammatoi*, could mean illiterate—literally, "without letters," that is, not knowing the ABCs. But whether Peter and John were or were not literate, there was no question, even in the minds of the sophisticated leaders of Jerusalem, that Peter and John had been with Jesus. The Jews had likewise marveled at Jesus, saying, "How does this Man know letters, having never studied?" (John 7:15).

The members of the Sanhedrin then went into a closed-door

session and made two decisions. One was to accept the validity of the miracle because, by then, virtually everyone in Jerusalem had heard of it. The word had spread as quickly as it would today, having made the 6:00 P.M. news. The second decision was to intimidate the apostles so their movement would spread no further.

If this was a closed-door session, how would Luke have known what they discussed? It could have been that Saul, later the apostle Paul, had been present because he had been a member of the Sanhedrin. He would later have told His companion, Luke.

But a further question arises: Why they did not attempt to refute the apostles' major claim—that Jesus had been raised from the dead? If they did, that would have stopped the movement without having to make an empty threat to Peter and John. For one thing, they had already debated it and bribed soldiers to lie about it, and that hadn't worked. It was a fact that Jesus had risen again. And for another thing, as we have seen, the Sadducees and Pharisees disagreed on the doctrine of the Resurrection in general, and they both knew that raising the issue in the Sanhedrin would have disrupted the meeting.

The Showdown

18. And they called them and commanded them not to speak at all nor teach in the name of Jesus. 19. But Peter and John answered and said to them, "Whether it is right in the sight of God to listen to you more than to God, you judge. 20. For we cannot but speak the things which we have seen and heard." 21. So...they let them go, finding no way of punishing them,...

Think of the scenario. Here was the Israeli Supreme Court—71 learned, bearded, cold-eyed, scowling rabbis calling in two hillbilly fishermen. No oddsmaker would have given the apostles the slightest chance of winning this showdown. The verdict was gravely announced with appropriate courtroom pomp and circumstance: No more preaching! Surprisingly, the apostles defied the Sanhedrin, perhaps realizing through the Holy Spirit that they had strong public opinion on their side. Their response might even have bordered on civil disobedience, but their priorities in desiring to serve God, no matter what, were straight. Realizing their bluff had been called, the authorities freed the apostles.

This episode, in my opinion, was the most significant event to date for the spread of the gospel among the Jews since Jesus had left the earth. Theologically, Pentecost may well have been more significant, but probably not strategically. This public test case involving the highest spiritual and religious authorities in first-century Judaism functionally cleared the way for the gospel to continue to spread through the Jewish community, both Hebrew and Hellenist, which it rapidly proceeded to do.

What Happened to the Church?

23. And being let go, they went to their own companions and reported all that the chief priests and elders had said to them. 24. So when they heard that, they raised their voice to God with one accord and said: "Lord, You are God, who made heaven and earth and the sea, and all that is in them, 29. Now, Lord, look on their threats, and grant to Your servants that with all boldness they may speak Your word, 30. by stretching out Your hand to heal, and that signs and wonders may be done through the name of Your holy Servant Jesus."

We do not know how many would have been in the group of

"companions" to whom Peter and John reported. This could well have been what we call today their "support group," made up most likely of some of those who were in the Upper Room on the Day of Pentecost. They, undoubtedly, had been praying through the trial, and when they heard the outcome, their immediate response was to lift their voices in corporate praise to the Lord of lords. They acknowledged the sovereignty of God who had prepared the way for Peter and John so that the Sanhedrin would **do whatever Your hand and Your purpose determined before to be done** (4:28). They prayed for the two major emphases of the whole book of Acts:

- Boldness to evangelize in Jerusalem, Judea, Samaria and to the end of the earth,
- Supernatural power in signs and wonders to accompany their ministry of evangelization.

God answered their prayer immediately, and visibly, because they obviously were praying according to His will:

31. And when they had prayed, the place where they were assembled together was shaken; and they were all filled with the Holy Spirit, and they spoke the word of God with boldness.

Reflection Questions

1. How do we explain that it is not exactly accurate to refer to the early believers in Jerusalem as "Christians"? What are more accurate terms?

2. The blind beggar received healing even though he didn't have faith. What are different ways that faith enters the healing process?

3. Why would the Sadducees—even more than the Pharisees—be so upset over what was happening in Jerusalem?

4. The Jerusalem church grew from 3,000 to 15,000 in three months. What would your community look like if the church increased fivefold in a short time?

5. The Sanhedrin ordered the apostles to stop preaching, but they ignored the order. Is this civil disobedience? Can such a thing be justified?

Notes

1. Otto Betz, "Exousia," *The New International Dictionary of New Testament Theology*, Colin Brown, ed. (Grand Rapids, MI: Zondervan Publishing House, 1976), Vol. 2, p. 607.

2. Richard B. Rackham, *The Acts of the Apostles: An Exposition* (London, England: Methuen & Co. Ltd., 1901), p. 44.

3. Donald A. Hagner, "Sadducees." Taken from the book, *The Zondervan Pictorial Encyclopedia of the Bible* by Merrill C. Tenney, ed. Copyright © 1975, 1976 by The Zondervan Corporation. Used by permission of Zondervan Publishing House. Vol. 5, p. 213.

4. Ibid., p. 214.

5. Rackham, *The Acts of the Apostles*, p. 45.

6. Hagner, "Sadducees," p. 215.

7. Ernst Haenchen, *The Acts of the Apostles: A Commentary* (Louisville, KY: Westminster Press, 1971), p. 189.

8. I. Howard Marshall, *Acts* (Grand Rapids, MI: William B. Eerdmans Publishing Co., 1980), p. 98.

9. F. F. Bruce, *The Book of Acts* (Grand Rapids, MI: William B. Eerdmans Publishing Co., 1988), p. 91. Used by permission.

10. Ibid.

11. Simon J. Kistemaker, *New Testament Commentary: Exposition on the Acts of the Apostles* (Grand Rapids, MI: Baker Book House Company, 1990), p. 151. Used by permission.

CHAPTER

6

Acts 4 and 5

Follow These Signs to Salvation

Acts 4 and 5

These were exciting days for those who had committed their lives to follow Jesus. By this time, they were beginning to feel that the kingdom of God was not going to be seriously restrained by worldly religious and political powers such as the Sanhedrin. The gates of Hades, as Jesus had said, were not going to stand in the way of the gospel. God had once again manifested Himself physically by shaking the room where the believers were praying (see Acts 4:31). Many newer believers were there this time who had not been present on the Day of Pentecost, but they saw and felt a very similar incident. Once again, they **were all filled with the Holy Spirit** (Acts 4:31).

After describing this remarkable event, Luke changes the pace and pauses, as he frequently does, to scan the broader picture. Here, Luke looks at the general behavior of this newborn first-century church and shows us how their lifestyle reflected the values of the kingdom of God. Their lives displayed what many call the "signs of the Kingdom."

The Signs of the Kingdom and the Blessing of God

Acts 4

....

32. Now the multitude of those who believed were of one heart and one soul; neither did anyone say that any of the things he possessed was his own, but they had all things in common. 33. And with great power the apostles gave witness to the resurrection of the Lord Jesus. And great grace was upon them all.

....

Right from the start, the believers had built two important things into their lifestyle: (1) they generously shared their material goods with one another, and (2) they witnessed with power. As a result, **great grace was upon them all.** God was responding to their service to Him by pouring out His blessing.

Both of these characteristics of the Jerusalem church are signs that the kingdom of God was present in their midst. They, of course, are not the only signs of the Kingdom, but they are important enough examples for Luke to occupy the rest of Acts 4 and all of chapter 5 in detailing how they were being implemented.

What Are "Signs of the Kingdom"?

Jesus said to His disciples, "And this gospel of the kingdom will be preached in all the world as a witness to all the nations, and then the end will come" (Matt. 24:14). The heart of the

Christian message is the kingdom of God. In the Lord's Prayer itself, we are supposed to pray, "Your kingdom come. Your will be done on earth as it is in heaven" (Matt. 6:10).

If this is what we preach about and pray about, how do we know if, and when, our prayers are being answered? We know by observing tangible signs of the Kingdom.

As we have seen on many occasions up to this point, the kingdom of God is not a sociopolitical kingdom. It is easy to fall into this kind of erroneous thinking, as we see from the disciples themselves. Even though, while He was on earth, Jesus took great pains to explain to His disciples and others that, "My kingdom is not of this world" (John 18:36), they did not fully understand it until long after He had left. As we saw in Acts 1, they were still saying, **"Lord, will You at this time restore the kingdom to Israel?"** (Acts 1:6). They were hoping that Jesus would liberate them from the political yoke of the Romans. In fact, this idea had contributed greatly to the strong opposition of the Sadducees who had been doing very well under the Romans and wished to preserve the status quo.

Unfortunately, this idea has not disappeared over 20 centuries. Many good-hearted Christians are still hoping wistfully that secular government will legislate the Ten Commandments and the Sermon on the Mount. They are saying, "Jesus, will you restore Your kingdom to our nation?" The desire that God's kingdom will come is commendable, but the thought that it will happen through sociopolitical mechanisms does not fit Jesus' teaching that His kingdom is not of this world.

The kingdom of God does not have geographical or political boundaries. It is present in the world through communities of believers who recognize Jesus Christ as the Lord of their lives and encourage the signs of the Kingdom to characterize their behavior both individually and collectively. This is exactly what the members of the Jerusalem church were doing in those early days.

When Jesus first began His public ministry, Matthew says that He preached, saying, "Repent, for the kingdom of heaven is at hand" (Matt. 4:17). One of the first places Jesus went was to His home town of Nazareth where He used the synagogue as His platform to make the first public announcement of His ministry agenda. As Luke adds details to this story (see Luke 4:16-19), he does not explicitly state that Jesus' agenda items are "signs of the Kingdom," but it is not at all out of line to surmise that they are exactly that. Here are these signs that, incidentally, were taken directly from the Old Testament in Isaiah 61:

1. Preaching the gospel to the poor.
2. Healing the brokenhearted.
3. Preaching deliverance to captives.
4. Restoring sight to the blind.
5. Liberating the oppressed.
6. Instituting the acceptable year of the Lord.

Through the years, as would be expected, these signs have been interpreted in a variety of ways. Some take them quite literally, while others strive to extract deeper spiritual meanings or see them as metaphors. My purpose at this point is not to discuss varieties of interpretations but simply to point out that whatever one's understanding of them might be, when these ministries characterize the behavior of Christians, God's kingdom is present.

But the list is longer. At one point, John the Baptist was downhearted and discouraged. He had also preached, "Repent, for the kingdom of heaven is at hand" (Matt. 3:2), but he wasn't seeing God's kingdom coming as rapidly and widely as he thought it should. So he got on Jesus' case by sending two of his own disciples to ask Jesus, "Are You the Coming One, or do we look for another?" (Luke 7:19). Jesus did not respond to this highly impertinent question with either a rebuke or a theological argument. He simply responded by listing some more of the tangible signs of the Kingdom that had been publicly visible through His ministry and by demonstrating them right before the eyes of John the Baptist's messengers (see Luke 7:20-23). Without repeating any of the signs already listed above, here are the additional ones:

7. Healing the sick.
8. Casting out evil spirits.
9. Making lame people walk.
10. Cleansing lepers.
11. Restoring hearing to the deaf.
12. Raising the dead.

When Jesus sent out His disciples to preach the gospel in all the world, He said that they would expect the signs of the Kingdom to follow them as they went (see Mark 16:15-18). Although some biblical scholars debate whether the original Greek text of Mark actually included this passage, most agree that the signs listed were, in fact, characteristic of the lifestyle of those who were preaching the gospel of the Kingdom in those days. We can therefore add:

13. Speaking in new tongues.
14. Safely picking up serpents (see Acts 28:3-5).
15. Immunity to poison.

These 15 signs of the Kingdom are by no means exhaustive. The New Testament is peppered with other significant characteristics of the lifestyle of Christians that just as clearly reflect the presence of the kingdom of God as do these. However, these 15 signs do give us a broad picture in which to understand Luke's description of how the believers in Jerusalem were working out some of them in their daily church life.

One of the Signs: Sharing Material Goods (Acts 4:34—5:11)

The last time Luke paused to describe the Church was after the Day of Pentecost. There he mentioned sharing material goods almost in passing (see Acts 2:44,45). Now he again describes the Church after an event, which in my mind ranks alongside of Pentecost in significance for advancing the Kingdom, and he also discloses how they were sharing material goods but this time in much more detail.

Sharing material goods is one of those signs of the Kingdom outside the list of 15 above. It characterizes those who have been **filled with the Holy Spirit** (Acts 4:31), as these believers were, because one of the fruits of the Holy Spirit is "goodness" (see Gal. 5:22). A clear Kingdom principle Jesus often taught was to regard material possessions as secondary. He said, "Do not lay up for yourselves treasures on earth, where moth and rust destroy and where thieves break in and steal" (Matt. 6:19). He also taught, "You shall love your neighbor as yourself" (Matt. 22:39).

Put these things together, and it is understandable why the believers in Jerusalem **did [not] say that any of the things [they] possessed was [their] own, but they had all things in common** (Acts 4:32).

The Kingdom principle is not to do without material goods. The principle is that we should not *prioritize* material goods. We should prioritize unselfishly loving our fellow believers and also our wider circle of neighbors whether they are Christians or not. This is what Jesus meant when He said, "Seek first the kingdom of God and His righteousness, and all these things shall be added to you" (Matt. 6:33). Here is another statement of priorities. If we prioritize the Kingdom and its values, we will not lack "all these things," which refers to material goods. In the Lord's Prayer, we first pray, "Your kingdom come," and then, "Give us this day our daily bread." The order is very important because it indicates the proper priorities. If we follow God's priorities, He will see that we are taken care of materially.

Putting the Principle into Practice

> 34. Nor was there anyone among them who lacked; for all who were possessors of lands or houses sold them, and brought the proceeds of the things that were sold, 35. and laid them at the apostles' feet; and they distributed to each as anyone had need.

The believers in Jerusalem decided to implement the principle of sharing material goods by selling real estate. Some modern readers stumble slightly at this passage because it seems to go against private ownership of land. But this is to confuse the *principle* with the *practice*. The principle is not private ownership of land but prioritizing the values of the kingdom of God, as we have seen. To these believers, material goods were secondary, as they should have been.

We need not conclude that *everyone* in the church sold *every* house or lot they possessed. Our translation, **all who were possessors of lands or houses sold them,** may not be the best way of understanding the underlying Greek text. For example, Simon Kistemaker translates it as, "Those who were the owners of lands or houses would periodically sell them."[1] This translation is much less problematical and helps put the practice of the principle more within the reach of our contemporary Christian community. Bible scholars generally agree that this is not some sort of appeal for a type of Christian communism because private ownership of property is affirmed both in the Old Testament and in the New Testament. For example, Mary the mother of Mark obviously kept her private house (see Acts 12:12).

Even so, the principle is a radical one. I like the way John Stott puts it: "Although in fact and in law they continued to own their goods, yet in heart and mind they cultivated an attitude so radical that they thought of their possessions as being available to help needy sisters and brothers."[2] The amazing result was that no poverty existed in the Church: **Nor was there anyone among them who lacked.**

Christians Should Not Be Poor

As I understand God's kingdom economy, nothing is wrong with having rich people in the Church, but something is wrong about having poor people in the Church. The Old Testament principle in Deuteronomy 15:4 states that there should be "no poor among you." The New Testament principle states that the gospel, or the "good news," should be preached to the poor (see Luke 4:18). When the people of God are **of one heart and one soul** (Acts 4:32), as they were in Jerusalem, implementing the principle of providing for the poor requires neither argument nor planning. It happens as naturally as a mother providing food for her baby.

I am appalled when I read the annual reports of the levels of giving in our American churches. No wonder we are not able to take care of our poor, even among our own church members. As I have mentioned before, the bare minimum for a Christian who desires a Kingdom lifestyle is 10 percent of income. In most American churches, however, the median giving is less than 3 percent. At this writing, our last four presidents all professed to be born-again Christians, yet the most one of them gave was 5 percent and the rest were all below that. Having such role models, it is not surprising that some modern Christians stumble when they are confronted with the radical example of the Jerusalem church.

Few of us may be ready to sell real estate in order to give tangible evidence that the Kingdom has come and that we have our priorities straight. However, if we simply started with a tithe, many of our church financial problems would be over, and we would be able to provide substantially for the poor. Another step in which I believe, and which my wife and I have practiced for almost 20 years, is the "graduated tithe," which means increasing the *percentage* of giving each year that God blesses with an increase of annual income. Ten percent has been left far behind, and so far, we are not lacking.

If we more diligently put the principle of sharing material possessions into practice, someone might be able to say about our church, **And great grace was upon them all** (Acts 4:33).

An Example: Barnabas

36. And Joses, who was also named Barnabas by the apostles (which is translated Son of Encouragement), a Levite of the country of Cyprus, 37. having land, sold it, and brought the money and laid it at the apostles' feet.

This is the first mention of Barnabas, who becomes a major character in the book of Acts and whom Luke mentions more than 20 times. In this story of how the signs of the Kingdom were being manifested in the Jerusalem church, Luke carefully selects Barnabas as a model of the believers. Barnabas provides for us a concrete example of how the principle of sharing material goods was being implemented, and later Ananias and Sapphira show how the same principle was violated. Luke characterizes Barnabas as **a good man, full of the Holy Spirit and of faith** (Acts 11:24). Here he lists three specific things about this remarkable man:

Barnabas was a Levite. This is of passing interest because, as some may recall, the Old Testament Levites were not supposed to own property (see Deut. 18:2), and they were given no territory in the Promised Land (see Josh. 13:14). However, as Everett Harrison points out, "Even by the time of Jeremiah this was not strictly maintained (Jer. 1:1; 32:6-15)."[3] This also serves to remind us that up to this point all the believers were still Jews, and among Jews, being a Levite was important enough to note even in a brief biographical sketch.

Barnabas was a Hellenistic Jew. I pointed out in chapter 2 that all 12 of Jesus' inner circle were Hebrew Jews. We do not know whether there were any exceptions to this among the 120 in the Upper Room on Pentecost, although Joseph Barsabas is thought by some to be a Cyprian, as was Barnabas. In any case, Barnabas is the first clearly Hellenistic Jew mentioned in Acts. These, as has been said, were born and raised outside of Palestine and were much more influenced by the prevailing Greek culture than were the Hebrews, and, therefore, they were called "Hellenists," a term that means "like the Greeks." It is important to keep in mind that Barnabas was not a Gentile but a racial Jew who also spoke Greek and, culturally, was somewhat different from the Hebrew Jews.

This difference becomes crucial when a conflict between the Hebrews and Hellenists erupts in Acts 6. In terms of selling private property, it is likely that the Hellenists would have been more affluent and thus would have owned more property than the Hebrew Jewish believers. (More on this in the next chapter.)

Barnabas was an encourager. The apostles thought so highly of this man whose name was Joses that they gave him a nickname, Barnabas, meaning Son of Encouragement. William LaSor says, "Barnabas was good at exhorting, encouraging, comforting. He must have been a wonderful man to have been given such a wonderful name!"⁴ It seems that Barnabas had a pastor's heart and was a phlegmatic personality type; quite a contrast from Paul with whom no small conflict arises almost 20 years later.

An Exception: Ananias and Sapphira
Acts 5

1. But a certain man named Ananias, with Sapphira his wife, sold a possession. 2. And he kept back part of the proceeds, his wife also being aware of it, and brought a certain part and laid it at the apostles' feet. 3. But Peter said, "Ananias, why has Satan filled your heart to lie to the Holy Spirit and keep back part of the price of the land for yourself? 4. While it remained, was it not your own? And after it was sold, was it not in your own control? Why have you conceived this thing in your heart? You have not lied to men but to God." 5. Then Ananias, hearing these words, fell down and breathed his last. So great fear came upon all those who heard these things. 6. And the young men arose and wrapped him up, carried him out, and buried him. 7. Now it was about three hours later when his wife came in, not knowing what had happened. 8. And Peter answered her, "Tell me whether you sold the land for so much?" And she said, "Yes, for so much." 9. Then Peter said to her, "How is it that you have agreed together to test the Spirit of the Lord? Look, the feet of those who have buried your husband are at the door, and they will carry you out." 10. Then immediately she fell down at his feet and breathed her last. And the young men came in and found her dead, and carrying her out, buried

her by her husband. 11. So great fear came upon all the church and upon all who heard these things.

Barnabas was the example of those who used the practice of selling property for God's glory, while Ananias and Sapphira are examples of those who attempted to use it to enhance their own reputation.

What was Ananias's and Sapphira's sin? A cursory reading might lead to the notion that their sin was withholding money and not giving enough to the church. But Peter clearly points out that Ananias had two other options he did not elect to take:

First, Ananias could have decided not to sell the property at all, but keep it for himself. **While it remained, was it not your own?** This is another indication that the Jerusalem church was not practicing a form of Christian communism because selling private property was regarded as a personal decision, not a requirement legislated by the church and imposed on its membership. Had Ananias and Sapphira chosen this option, they certainly would not have received God's death penalty.

Second, Ananias could have sold the property and made a partial donation to the church. **"And after it was sold, was it not in your own control?"** If he would have done this aboveboard, presumably, he would not have been rebuked.

Instead, Ananias and Sapphira made the decision to lie to the church in order to make themselves appear as committed to God's kingdom and its priorities as Barnabas and others were. Big mistake! Stinginess could have been tolerated, but not hypocrisy. Ananias's intentional, premeditated deception was seen as a more serious sin than usual: **You have not lied to men but to God.**

"The Devil Made Me Do It!"
What caused Ananias and Sapphira to do this? Obviously, Satan

had something to do with it because Peter says, **"Why has Satan filled your heart?"** At this point, Peter was talking from personal experience. When Peter had rebuked Jesus on one occasion, Jesus said, "Get behind me, Satan" (Matt. 16:23).

Peter had learned personally that he could not excuse his own moral lapses before God by saying, "The devil made me do it." Although Satan certainly was behind Ananias's deception, Ananias couldn't blame his misbehavior on Satan. He himself was the one who had lied to the Holy Spirit, and he was the one who subsequently received the judgment of God.

Ananias could have resisted Satan's temptation, as can any believer in such a situation. James says, "Resist the devil and he will flee from you" (Jas. 4:7). Paul asserts that God provides ways of escape with each temptation, and that the choice to take the way of escape or not is ours (see 1 Cor. 10:13).

This is not to ignore the fact that Satan has gained more control over some believers than others. Although it is not theologically sound to suppose that a Christian can be demon *possessed*, it is clear that demonization can occur at least to the extent of Satan "filling the heart," as in the case of Ananias. Some are more comfortable with the terms "demonic oppression" or "demonic affliction," while others transliterate the Greek and use "demonization." All are attempts to acknowledge that Satan goes about like a roaring lion, seeking whom he may devour (see 1 Pet. 5:8).

Even in cases of severe demonization, more frequently than not, the believer has given Satan a legal ground, or a stronghold, from which to operate. Peter's question to Ananias, **"Why has Satan filled your heart?"** carries the clear implication that Ananias somehow had allowed him to do it. Now he was paying the consequences, and his wife, who had joined him in the plot, would soon follow suit.

Some may be asking how curses relate to this. It is true that believers can also be victimized through satanic attack, as was Job. But although powers of darkness can influence health, loved ones, material possessions and peace, *moral decisions* are the responsibility of the individual. Satan can deceive us, but he cannot make our moral choices. Although Job was a victim of almost every conceivable direct attack of Satan, in moral issues he maintained his uprightness and did not sin (see Job 1:22; 2:3,10). Ananias could have done the same but chose not to.

Hearing from God

How did Peter know that Ananias was lying?

As I study the commentaries on this passage, I am rather fascinated at how few commentators raise this question. Of course, there could have been some natural explanations. Ananias may have been one of those poor liars who can't help but give it away. Or Peter may have received some insider information about the real estate deal before Ananias showed up. As I read it, however, the whole tone of the passage seems to indicate that something much more supernatural is behind this event.

Although I cannot prove it directly from the text, I have a hunch that if someone had asked Peter how he knew, he would have said, "God told me." It is not out of line to suppose that we have here an example of New Testament prophecy (see 1 Cor. 14:24,25). Peter, filled with the Holy Spirit, had his ear carefully tuned to receiving revelation from God that was directly applicable to the situation. Stanley Horton agrees when he says, "Perhaps this was revealed to him through one of the gifts of revelation."[5]

This is how Peter would also have known that God was going to apply capital punishment. The sentence of death was not from Peter, it was from God. Although Luke does not record that Peter spoke the sentence to Ananias, it is clearly recorded that he did speak it to his wife, Sapphira (see Acts 5:9).

I believe that one of the main lessons of this dramatic passage is that the Holy Spirit is a real person and that He is directly in touch with the Church and with every individual member.

Speaking of the Church, Luke ends this story by saying: **So great fear came upon all the church.** This is the first use of the technical term "church" from the Greek *ekklesia* in the book of Acts, but it is subsequently used 22 more times. Some may say: How about Acts 2:47, where we read, **And the Lord added to the church daily those who were being saved?** The Greek term *ekklesia* does not appear in this verse, and many modern translations reflect this by saying, "the Lord added to *their number*" rather than to "*the church*."

Another Sign of the Kingdom: Power Ministry (Acts 5:12-42)

The theme of this chapter is the signs of the kingdom of God, which, as true signs do, point to a destination. For the book of Acts that destination is salvation spreading from Jerusalem to Judea, Samaria and the end of the earth. Although the Church and the kingdom of God are not one and the same, churches that do display the signs of the Kingdom bring the two together here on earth.

We have seen that one of the signs of the Kingdom clearly displayed in the church in Jerusalem was a willingness to share their material goods, particularly with the poor. Another sign was their active involvement in what we call today "power ministries." For example, when Jesus healed a blind and mute man by casting out a demon, He explained, "But if I cast out demons by the Spirit of God, surely the kingdom of God has come upon you" (Matt. 12:28). How do we know that the kingdom of God is authentically among us? One way is to see healings and demonic deliverances as part of the ministry of the Church.

Quantity and Quality

Church growth needs to take place both in quantity and quality. Luke seems to realize this as he weaves them together in these first few chapters of Acts:

- *Quality* in Acts 1. Here we observe the believers in prayer and in organizing themselves by appointing Matthias as Judas's replacement.
- *Quantity* in Acts 2:1-41. The Day of Pentecost sees 3,000 come to Christ.
- *Quality* in Acts 2:42-47. The church continues stead fast and shares their material goods.
- *Quantity* in Acts 3:1—4:22. The lame man is healed and the church grows to 15,000.
- *Quality* in Acts 4:23—5:11. Believers pray and share their material possessions.
- *Quantity* in Acts 5:12-42. Signs and wonders point the way to salvation for many.
- *Quality* in Acts 6:1-6. Reorganization of the church.
- *Quantity* in Acts 6:7. Many priests are converted.

Sharing material goods can be seen as a sign of the Kingdom that contributes to internal growth or to the *quality* of the church. In contrast, the signs and wonders and power ministry seem to point more to the outward ministry to the world and, therefore, to *quantitative* church growth. Both are needed.

The Miracles and Wonders

....

12. And through the hands of the apostles many signs and wonders were done among the people. And they were all

with one accord in Solomon's Porch. 13. Yet none of the
rest dared join them, but the people esteemed them highly.
14. And believers were increasingly added to the Lord,
multitudes of both men and women, 15. so that they
brought the sick out into the streets and laid them on beds
and couches, that at least the shadow of Peter passing by
might fall on some of them. 16. Also a multitude gathered
from the surrounding cities to Jerusalem, bringing sick
people and those who were tormented by unclean spirits,
and they were all healed.

....

The parallel with Acts 2 continues. There, **they were all filled
with the Holy Spirit** (2:4) and here, **they were all filled with
the Holy Spirit** (4:31). There, God sent a tangible **sound from
heaven, as of a rushing mighty wind** (2:2), and here, **the place
where they were assembled together was shaken** (4:31). There,
they **sold their possessions and goods, and divided them among
all** (2:45), and here, they sold their possessions and **had all things
in common** (4:32). There, **many wonders and signs were done
through the apostles** (2:43), and here, **through the hands of the
apostles many signs and wonders were done among the people**
(Acts 5:12).

Luke is also anxious to remind us that the purpose for all this
was the spread of the gospel and the salvation of souls. There, **the
Lord added to the church daily those who were being saved**
(2:47), and here, **believers were increasingly added to the Lord,
multitudes of both men and women** (5:14).

The title of this chapter, "Follow These Signs to Salvation," is
meant to point out that the signs of the kingdom of God have as
their major purpose to bring glory to God through the salvation
of the lost. At this point, we are dealing with **many signs and
wonders.** These signs and wonders are to be seen as one of the

manifestations of receiving **power when the Holy Spirit has come upon you,** to repeat the last words of Jesus spoken in Acts 1:8. Because Acts 1:8 is the acknowledged table of contents for the book of Acts, the working of the Holy Spirit through power ministries needs to be understood as thoroughly as possible.

Paradigm Shifts

Many Christians today, particularly those of us not rooted in Pentecostal or charismatic traditions, have had to make major adjustments to the restoration of ministries of the miraculous spreading throughout the whole Body of Christ beginning in the 1980s. Most of us, including myself, have had to go through paradigm shifts in order to adjust our thinking, our attitudes and our ministry to what for us is a new spiritual reality. Although we previously read and believed the Acts of the Apostles, the stories of signs and wonders we found there seemed rather misty, relegated to something that might have occurred in the distant past or something that might yet be occurring on a far-off mission field but with little relevance to mainstream United States Christianity. Some of us might even have thought that our superior version of Christianity was mature enough and sophisticated enough so that these rather primitive manifestations were no longer needed.

A major factor in stimulating traditional evangelical paradigm shifts was the leadership of John Wimber, who began his own paradigm shift around 1978. Wimber systematized his theories by teaching the much-publicized Fuller Seminary course "MC510: Signs, Wonders and Church Growth" for several years. He developed the practice through founding the Vineyard Christian Fellowship of Anaheim, California, which rapidly became one of America's most outstanding megachurches.

A corresponding body of literature sprang up. Wimber's ideas are summarized in his books *Power Evangelism* (HarperCollins) and *Power Healing* (HarperCollins). As he was teaching at Fuller, two School of World Mission faculty members became Wimber disciples, went through their personal paradigm shifts and wrote books of their own. Charles Kraft, from the Evangelical Covenant Church, wrote *Christianity with Power* (Servant Publications), and I, from the Congregational Church, wrote *How to Have a Healing Ministry in Any Church.* Many other books, also written by those outside the Pentecostal and charismatic traditions, have been added. In order to label this new phenomenon, some are using the term "Third Wave."

This dynamic contemporary movement is allowing us to understand the book of Acts in ways not reflected in the standard commentaries published before the emergence of the Third Wave, predictable exceptions being the Assemblies of God scholar Stanley Horton.

The Facts About Signs and Wonders

In order to understand this phenomenon of ministries in the miraculous, which will continue through the book of Acts, I am going to set forth some facts, then move on to interpretation.

First, power ministry was common. **And through the hands of the apostles many signs and wonders were done among the people** (5:12). The signs and wonders, of course, didn't start here. The lame man at the Temple gate had been healed. Signs and wonders are mentioned in Acts 2. And many had been healing the sick and casting out demons while Jesus was still on earth (see Mark 9:38,39; Luke 9:49,50; 10:1,9).

Second, sick people from surrounding areas were brought into Jerusalem for the specific purpose of receiving divine healing and deliverance from demonic spirits (see 5:16). This seems to be significant from the evangelistic point of view. Presumably, those who had been healed by the power of God later returned to their homes and testified of their healing and of Jesus as Messiah. Because they likely would have come from many parts of Judea, they probably would have become the major carriers of the gospel from "Jerusalem to Judea" as Jesus had mandated in Acts 1:8. Previously, from what we know, the gospel would have been limited largely to Jerusalem and Galilee, the province to the north where most of Jesus' earthly ministry had taken place.

How the gospel could have spread through the testimony of these simple believers, without prestigious apostles and other leaders accompanying them, can be clearly understood by observing the rapid spread of Christianity throughout mainland China today. My friend, David Wang of Asian Outreach, helped me through my paradigm shift in the early 1980s by bringing me firsthand reports of multitudes of simple Chinese people coming to Christ through signs and wonders.

Wang told, for example, of a commune of more than 30,000 that remarkably was all Christian. The commune had become known as "Yesu Mountain." The Christian church there for years had been small and struggling, virtually throttled by an aggressive communist party leader from Beijing. Then the communist official developed advanced cancer in his nose that was beyond the scope of medical science. In desperation and in fear of losing his life, he swallowed his pride and asked the Christian leader he had been persecuting to pray to God for healing. The cancer was totally cured, the man became a believer and the way was opened for a people movement that swept the whole commune. The officer was subsequently jailed but rejoiced for the privilege of suffering for Christ, as did many in the book of Acts (see Acts 5:41).

Throughout China today, such stories are almost as common as chopsticks. As a result, at this writing, an estimated 35,000 Chinese are becoming Christians every single day. In sheer magnitude, it dwarfs anything Luke could have possibly imagined.

Third, **They brought the sick out into the streets...that at least the shadow of Peter passing by might fall on some of them (5:15).** Apparently Peter, at the time, was ministering in the role of what some would call a "faith healer" today. Others were doing miracles as well, but it seems that Peter had the special anointing. In fact, it was so powerful that some were healed simply through being near him even though they received no personal ministry or prayer. Although it is unusual both yesterday and today, nevertheless, similar things are being reported in our times. Personal friends of mine, such as Cindy Jacobs, Reinhart Bonnke and John Wimber, have experienced anointings seemingly as powerful as Peter's.

Interpreting the Facts

My intention in this section is not to repeat the material on signs and wonders covered in books such as those referenced previously, but rather in a limited space to help those readers who may be considering a paradigm shift. Such a shift will greatly enhance our ability to apply what we learn from the book of Acts to Christian life and ministry today. I realize this is not for everyone.

For example, one of the commentators I am using says, after describing some biblical miracles, "We should not, therefore, expect to do these things ourselves today....Even the healing miracles of the Gospels and Acts had features which are seldom manifested even in the signs and wonders movement today." My information leads me to a different conclusion. Evidence from many parts of the world points to the literal fulfillment of Jesus' words: "He who believes in Me, the works that I do he will do also; and greater works than these he will do, because I go to my Father" (John 14:12).

What Is the Purpose of Miracles?

It is important to understand, first of all, what miracles *are not*. They *are not*:

- For public display or curiosity, like a circus act, to arouse astonishment;
- To bring personal status or gain to the "faith healer" or to other Christians whom God uses to heal the sick;
- A form of Christian magic by which we manipulate the supernatural;
- Exclusively psychosomatic in their operation.

On the other hand, miracles *are*:

- Signs of the presence of the kingdom of God, as I have extensively argued;
- Expressions of God's compassion to alleviate those who are sick, in pain or demonized;
- Signs pointing to the power of Jesus Christ and His cross to save unbelievers, as Luke reports in Acts 5:14.

How Many for Whom We Pray Are Actually Healed?

Luke reports that the multitude of people who came into Jerusalem **were all healed** (5:16). For those of us who are attempting to practice power ministries today, this is extraordinary. Hermeneutically speaking, the word "all" does not always have to mean "every single one without exception." But I know of no good reason to doubt that in this case every single one was, in fact, healed. For one thing, it would mean that Peter's shadow itself was one of the effective instruments of healing. This was certainly a notable occurrence.

In most cases we know of today not everyone is healed, even in meetings where a special anointing seems to come. When I began my healing ministry, I supplied report forms to each person I prayed for over a five-year period. Generally speaking, 25 percent to 30 percent were completely healed, 50 percent to 60 percent reported some healing and around 20 percent sensed no improvement. I have compared these findings with other healing ministries and found comparable outcomes. I believe we should aim for the 100 percent healing we find in Acts 5:16, but I also believe that, meanwhile, we should glorify God for the healing that does take place through prayer and the power of the Holy Spirit even if all are not healed.

We can take some comfort in the fact that Jesus Himself did not heal every sick or demonized person He met. When Jesus returned to His hometown of Nazareth, "He did not do many mighty works there because of their unbelief" (Matt. 13:58). At the pool of Bethesda, Jesus found a great multitude of sick people but healed only one of them (see John 5:1-9). And as I mentioned previously, Jesus must have passed by the lame beggar at the Temple gate many times, but the healing came later through Peter and John (see Acts 3:1-11).

How Long Did Those Who Were Healed Stay Well?

We have no report of the answer to the question of how long those who were healed stayed well, but one thing we do know— they all eventually died. It is good to keep in mind that healing is extremely valuable, but it is only temporal. That is why Jesus reminded His disciples, after a powerful healing campaign, that more important than the healing is to have one's name written in heaven (see Luke 10:20). Ministries in the miraculous, as I like to say, are only the *signs* pointing to the *Son*. The most important thing is salvation, and that is why Luke constantly reiterates that lost people were being saved.

Did Only the Apostles Have Healing Power?

In Acts 2:43 we read: **And many wonders and signs were done through the apostles.** Then, in Acts 4:33: **With great power the apostles gave witness.** And, here in Acts 5:12: **And through the hands of the apostles many signs and wonders were done among the people.** In light of this, one unnamed commentator says that such healings "were never intended for the church at large."

It is true that in his book The Acts of the Apostles, Luke has a great deal to say about the apostles' healing ministry. But as I read the New Testament, there is no intention to confine healing to the 12. Jesus demonstrated this by sending out 70 on ministries of healing and casting out demons in Luke 10. In Acts itself, Stephen, who was not an apostle, **did great wonders and signs among the people** (Acts 6:8). Also, multitudes listened to Philip's preaching, **seeing the miracles which he did** (Acts 8:6). Jesus expected that those who believe will "lay hands on the sick, and they will recover" (Mark 16:18). Later, the apostle Paul lists "gifts of healings" among the spiritual gifts God distributes throughout the Body of Christ (see 1 Cor. 12:9).

The Upshot? Back to Jail! (Acts 5:17-32)

17. **Then the high priest rose up, and all those who were with him (which is the sect of the Sadducees), and they were filled with indignation, 18. and laid their hands on the apostles and put them in the common prison.**

The Sadducees once again led the persecution. One of the reasons was that larger crowds were now listening to the apostles **giving witness to the resurrection of the Lord Jesus** (Acts

4:33), contradicting the Sadducees' teaching that there was no possibility of resurrection. Furthermore, they feared major social disruption emerging from the growing Messianic Jewish move- ment in Jerusalem. It is interesting that the rival sect of Pharisees did not share the depth of feeling with the Sadducees on either of these issues.

Apparently, several apostles, perhaps all 12, were arrested this time, not just Peter and John, as previously.

---

19. But at night an angel of the Lord opened the prison doors and brought them out, and said, 20. "Go, stand in the temple and speak to the people all the words of this life." 21. And when they heard that, they entered the temple early in the morning and taught....

Some commentators find this story of an angelic visit a bit far fetched and affirm that it must have been a human messenger. I like Everett Harrison's reply: "While it is true that the word for 'angel' can also mean 'messenger' and indicate a human being, this is rare; it is wholly unlikely in the present instance, where the full description 'angel of the Lord' emphasizes celestial origin and dignity."[6]

Miracles are not always done by human agents, although this is the most common pattern in the New Testament. They are also done by angels, as in this case, and by direct, divine interven- tion, as Saul of Tarsus later experienced on the Damascus Road.

The angel commanded the apostles to disobey the Sanhedrin and to preach the gospel in the Temple. In a case such as this, whom do we obey? Is civil disobedience ever justified? We will focus on more of this shortly.

Arrested Once More!

....

24. Now when the high priest, the captain of the temple,
and the chief priests heard these things, they wondered
what the outcome would be. 25. Then one came and told
them, saying, "Look, the men whom you put in prison are
standing in the temple and teaching the people!"
26. Then the captain went with the officers and
brought them without violence, for they feared the
people, lest they should be stoned.

....

It is well to remember that the Sanhedrin was the supreme court
of Israel. This must have been an extremely embarrassing
moment for them—not a good day! The same authorities who
arrested Peter and John came again for the 12. This time, Luke
takes pains to mention that they did not use force in the arrest.
Why? By now, large numbers of people were getting healed, and,
therefore, they loved and owed a great deal to the apostles. The
authorities were afraid of being stoned, a fear that we can well
appreciate through frequent television news reports of distur-
bances in Israel today.

....

27. ...And the high priest asked them, 28, saying, "Did we
not strictly command you not to teach in this name? And
look, you have filled Jerusalem with your doctrine, and
intend to bring this Man's blood on us!"

....

The issue of civil disobedience is now coming to a head. And
a new underlying fear is surfacing—what would happen if the
people of Jerusalem blamed the Sanhedrin for the death of Jesus?
Even if Luke hadn't told us directly about the rapid growth of the
church in Jerusalem during these days, the statement of the high

priest about filling **Jerusalem with [the apostles'] doctrine** would suffice as a word of encouragement for Christian readers.

> 29. Then Peter and the other apostles answered and said:
> "We ought to obey God rather than men. 30. The God of
> our fathers raised up Jesus whom you murdered by hang-
> ing on a tree. 31. Him God has exalted to His right hand
> to be Prince and Savior, to give repentance to Israel and
> forgiveness of sins. 32. And we are His
> witnesses to these things,...

I know of Christian leaders today who are very critical of government officials, until they get invited to meet them personally. Then they change their tune. Not Peter! He directly accused them of murdering Jesus, reaffirmed the Resurrection and announced that he would engage in civil disobedience and obey God rather than the Sanhedrin. With this direct challenge to their authority, it is perfectly understandable why they wanted to kill the apostles.

The Verdict

> 33. When they heard this, they were furious and took
> counsel to kill them. 34. Then one in the council stood
> up, a Pharisee named Gamaliel, a teacher of the law held
> in respect by all the people,... 35. And he said to them:
> "Men of Israel, take heed to yourselves what you intend
> to do regarding these men. 38. And now I say to you,
> keep away from these men and let them alone; for if this
> plan or this work is of men, it will come to nothing;

> **39. but if it is of God, you cannot overthrow it—lest you even be found to fight against God."**

Luke seems to make the point that God's wisdom was given to the Sanhedrin through a Pharisee who was unafraid to confront the majority Sadducees. Gamaliel was a man of great respect, the chief mentor of Saul of Tarsus before he became the apostle Paul (see Acts 22:3). Gamaliel's wise counsel became crucial to maintaining the momentum of the early Christian movement.

> **40. And they agreed with him, and when they had called for the apostles and beaten them, they commanded that they should not speak in the name of Jesus, and let them go.**

Unfortunately for the apostles, the Sanhedrin took only part of Gamaliel's advice. Instead of leaving them completely alone, they had them beaten. This would ordinarily have been a severe physical punishment, but given the mood of the general public in Jerusalem at the time, one wonders whether the beating might have been more of the token variety.

> **41. So they departed from the presence of the council, rejoicing that they were counted worthy to suffer shame for His name. 42. And daily in the temple, and in every house, they did not cease teaching and preaching Jesus as the Christ.**

Whatever the punishment, the apostles' reaction was joy. The crucial event was over. The supreme court had caused the apostles to pay their debt to society for their perceived criminal actions. And now, much to the consternation of the Sadducees in particular, the apostles disobeyed their command not to preach and continued to spread the word about Jesus with relative impunity. The gospel of Christ had now become firmly planted in the social soil of the city of Jerusalem, and it would continue to bear much fruit for nearly 40 more years.

Reflection Questions

1. Look over the list of the 15 different signs of the kingdom of God. Which of the signs are evident in your church? Would you desire that the others become evident as well?
2. Very few Christians today go as far as to sell their real estate and give the proceeds to the church. Are there other ways that the same kind of dedication can be and is being shown?
3. Ananias committed a sin that cost his life. Satan had filled his heart. Why couldn't he blame his own failure on Satan?
4. The Church should grow both in quantity and quality. Review some of the ways we have seen both of them happen so far in Acts.
5. Supernatural signs and wonders were a vital part of the ministry of the apostles. Why do you think some would say that we shouldn't expect them today?

Notes

1. Simon J. Kistemaker, *New Testament Commentary: Exposition on the Acts of the Apostles* (Grand Rapids, MI: Baker Book House Company, 1990), p. 174. Used by permission.

2. John Stott, *The Spirit, The Church and the World* (Downers Grove, IL: InterVarsity Press, 1990), p. 107.
3. Everett F. Harrison, *Acts: The Expanding Church* (Chicago, IL: Moody Press, 1975), p. 91.
4. William Sanford LaSor, *Church Alive* (Ventura, CA: Regal Books, 1972), p. 73.
5. Stanley M. Horton, *The Book of Acts* (Springfield, MO: Gospel Publishing House, 1981), p. 72.
6. Harrison, *Acts*, p. 98.

CHAPTER

7

Acts 6

Should Foreigners Run the Church?

Acts 6

A great deal happens in the first seven verses of Acts 6 that has important implications for the subsequent expansion of the entire Christian movement. Back in chapter 2, I pointed out how the "people approach to world evangelization" has now been adopted by missiologists all over the world. Acts 6 gives us insight into this by letting us know for the first time that not one but two people groups had been mixed together in the local church in Jerusalem. What began as a monocultural church had suddenly become a bicultural church.

How the Holy Spirit led the apostles to handle this situation is a valuable lesson in dealing with cross-cultural situations wherever and whenever they occur in the Church or in missions. The application we shall draw from in these seven verses is missiological in nature. As a reminder, my highest priority in attempting this modern commentary on the book of Acts is not to replace the standard commentaries, but to supplement them in the areas of our contemporary knowledge of power ministries and missiology. The last chapter emphasized power ministries, while this one will emphasize missiology or key principles to be applied to cross-cultural ministries.

Restructuring the Church

The more bicultural the church at Jerusalem became, the more obvious it was that some radical changes in its structure needed to be considered. As Luke steps back, so to speak, to take another broad look at the church, he stresses two things: the numbers, as he usually does, and also the ethnic or cultural composition of the church.

Who's Counting?

1. Now in those days, when the number of the disciples was multiplying,...

Luke uses a different word to describe the growth of the church here, quite possibly reflecting an increasing *rate* of growth. Although the literal meaning of the Greek words cannot be pushed too far in this direction, nevertheless, the English words in our *New King James Version* say it clearly. In Acts 2:47 and 5:14 the Lord **added** those who were being saved, and here the number **was multiplying**. Growth by addition apparently became growth by multiplication. It was the same as compounding interest; the increasing numbers of disciples moving out in witness, presumably with power evangelism.

How many were there by this time?

This is the fifth church-growth report given so far by Luke.

The first, in Acts 2:41, gave us the number of 3,000. The second, in Acts 2:47, says more were added without a specific number. The third, in Acts 4:4, mentions 5,000 men, and at that point I suggested that a very conservative estimate would be a total of 15,000. The fourth, in Acts 5:14, still uses the word **added**, to indicate that large numbers of both men and women became believers. Acts 6:1 is the fifth report. R. C. H. Lenski says, "It has been conservatively estimated that at this time the total number of the disciples was between twenty and twenty-five thousand."[1] As I have mentioned, it is not necessary to imagine that 25,000 were in the city of Jerusalem itself, although they might have been.

In my opinion, it is important to notice that Luke regularly reports church growth. I say that because many Christian leaders today tend to scorn the use of numbers. Some label reporting growth as "triumphalism." Others say, "We're not interested in the numbers game." A common cliché goes: "We strive for quality, not quantity." I have even heard the use of numbers called "numerolatry," a particularly serious accusation because it implies a form of idolatry. Should Luke be charged with numerolatry because he shows interest in numbers?

I think it is safe to assume that Luke was not committing idolatry nor engaging in triumphalism by his frequent reporting of church growth, often with specific numbers. Although I would agree that some abuse numbers these days, others do not. David gives us an example of abuse. In 1 Chronicles 21:1 we read, "Now Satan stood up against Israel, and moved David to number Israel." David did this for his own glory and soon found it was a major mistake. "I have done very foolishly," he later said (1 Chron. 21:8). But, on the other hand, God, not Satan, said to Moses, "Take a census of all the congregation of the children of Israel" (Num. 1:2). So counting, in and of itself, is obviously not contrary to God's nature.

Church-growth expert Donald McGavran says, "The numerical approach is essential to understanding church growth. The church is made up of countable people and there is nothing particularly spiritual in not counting them."[2] I agree, and find it particularly encouraging that Luke apparently does also.

A Bicultural Church

··

**1. ...there arose a murmuring against the Hebrews
by the Hellenists,...**

··

Keep in mind that all the believers at this point were still Jews. No Samaritans or Gentiles had yet been brought into the fold. Whereas, this will soon change, the apostles were still following the direction Jesus gave them, "Do not go into the way of the Gentiles, and do not enter a city of the Samaritans, but go rather to the lost sheep of the house of Israel" (Matt. 10:5,6). They knew that eventually they would be making disciples of *all nations* (see Matt. 28:19), and that the gospel would move from Jerusalem to Judea out to Samaria and the end of the earth as Jesus had told them (see Acts 1:8), but the time for that had not yet come.

One reason it had not come, I believe, is that the original apostles, who were all Hebrew Jews, had not as yet learned how to relate properly to a culture much more akin to their own, namely, Hellenistic Jews. If they could not relate well to the Hellenists, how could they possibly relate to the much despised Samaritans or Gentiles? A problem had surfaced regarding widows, which I will describe later on. But we must keep in mind that this was only superficial. I agree with Howard Marshall who says, "The complaint about the poor relief was but a symptom of a deeper problem, namely that the Aramaic-speaking Christians and the Greek-speaking Christians were dividing into two separate groups."[3]

As one small indicator that something very significant is at stake here, Luke not only tells us that disciples were multiplying at the beginning of the incident, but only six verses later, after it is resolved, he repeats it even more enthusiastically (see Acts 6:7).

In order to understand the underlying dynamics, we need to understand the characteristics of each of these two ethnic groups.

The Hebrews

As I have pointed out more than once, all the original followers of Jesus were Hebrew Jews. In fact, up to the Day of Pentecost they were, with few possible exceptions, all *Galilean* Hebrews as opposed to *Judean* Hebrews. Remember that the Galileans were regarded as the first-century equivalent of hillbillies. On the Day of Pentecost, the more sophisticated Judeans in their own city of Jerusalem exclaimed with no little astonishment, **"Look, are not all these who speak Galileans?"** (Acts 2:7).

However, by the time we arrive at this passage in Acts 6, many of the believers were Judeans as well. Particularly in the great healing campaign where even Peter's shadow was healing the sick, a considerable number had come into Jerusalem from surrounding towns in Judea and had been healed and saved (see Acts 5:15,16). We can safely presume, therefore, that by this time the majority of the Hebrew believers in Jerusalem would have been Judeans. Although, undoubtedly, many other groups of Galileans were also followers of Jesus up north in their own province of Galilee.

The Hebrews spoke Aramaic as their mother tongue, a language closely related to Hebrew. Some of the better educated ones would also speak Greek, which was the trade language of most of the Roman Empire in those days. They read their Old

Testaments in the original Hebrew. They worshiped regularly in the Temple and provided the Temple priests.

It is easy to understand how the Hebrews would, and did, think of themselves as spiritually superior to the Hellenists. Even in the church, this attitude could have carried over and contributed to the friction that had developed between the two groups.

The Hellenists

The Hellenists were Greek-speaking Jews. The Greeks' own word for their native land of Greece is *Hellas*, a word derived from a Greek deity named Hellen, a son of Zeus. So "Hellenists," as applied to Jews, would mean "like the Greeks." They belonged to what is known as the "Jewish dispersion," meaning the migration of Jewish families from their original homeland in Palestine to various other nations of the ancient world. Most large cities of the Roman Empire would have a Jewish community, and it would not be uncommon to find a synagogue among them.

Although they spoke Greek as a trade language, their mother tongue would more likely be the regional dialect of the city or area where they and their families lived, much as the Italian community in Philadelphia today speaks English as their first language, although many can communicate in Italian as well. However, the important thing to keep in mind is that the Hellenists did not typically speak fluent Aramaic unless they had lived back in Jerusalem for some time. They did not read their Old Testaments in Hebrew but in the Greek translation called the Septuagint.

Up to the Day of Pentecost, Hellenists, even though they were full-blooded Jews, had not become followers of Jesus as their Messiah. There may have been an exception or two, such as Joseph Barsabas who was among the 120 in the Upper Room and also became a candidate for the twelfth apostle (see Acts 1:23), but these were few and far between. Therefore, when we get to Acts 6, we can understand that because virtually none of the Hellenists would have had a personal memory of Jesus Himself, as did many Hebrews, they might easily succumb to a spiritual inferiority complex when they were around the Hebrews. This caused a problem.

Why were so many Hellenists in Jerusalem? Crowds of them visited regularly for special feast occasions such as Pentecost, as we have seen. But why would some move there to live and, therefore, be considered a part of the church of the city?

Simon Kistemaker suggests that "many of these devout Jews were elderly people who wanted to spend the rest of their lives in the holy city."[4] If this is true, it would follow that of the millions of Jews throughout the dispersion, only the most affluent among them would be able to realize their dreams of finishing their days and being buried in Jerusalem. Therefore, the Hellenists in the church would likely be better off financially than the Hebrews on the average. In fact, all those actually mentioned by name as selling property to distribute to the poor were Hellenists, such as Barnabas who was from Cyprus (see Acts 4:36,37). Jerusalem must have been the Miami Beach of the first century, the place where many wealthy Jews go to retire and live out their days.

The Hellenistic Jews also went to Jerusalem for a theological reason. Messianic hopes for centuries, in Israel, projected the Messiah's arrival in the holy city of Jerusalem. Even today a visitor to Jerusalem is surprised to see the many burial grounds just outside the walls. Lively belief in resurrection yielded the confident hope of being on hand when Messiah would come.

Varieties of Hellenists

Even more significant for understanding Acts 6 is that when a considerable number of Hellenistic Jews in Jerusalem came from one particular region of the Roman Empire and spoke a common dialect, these families would naturally form their primary social groups with each other, not with those Hellenists who spoke other dialects, much less Aramaic-speaking Hebrews. In recent years, for example, many Russian Jews have moved to Los Angeles, and they prefer to socialize more with themselves than with fellow Jews who have been in America for generations. In fact, Kistemaker says, "Each group had its own synagogue before these people became Christians," and he points out that they maintained these language assemblies even after they had become disciples.[5]

In modern categories, we can usefully think of the Hellenistic Jews in Jerusalem as hyphenated ethnics. Whereas, for example, we have many Chinese in the United States, the Chinese do not regard themselves as belonging to the same *primary* group. They will easily mix together in public gatherings on Chinese New Year or to support favorable political causes, but these, similar to going to the Temple in Jerusalem, are *secondary* groups, sociologically speaking. When it comes to *primary* groups, Taiwanese-Chinese, Mainland-Chinese, Hong Kong-Chinese and Malaysian-Chinese, to cite obvious examples, tend not to associate with each other, even though they might reside in the same American neighborhood. Most of them can speak some English, but Taiwanese or Cantonese or Mandarin is the preferred language for their more intimate socializing.

Being good Jews, the Hellenists would also be Temple attenders, which should be seen as a secondary group. But their primary group remained the synagogue. According to the Talmud, Jerusalem had 480 synagogues at the time. Some of these are named later in Acts 6:9 as the **Synagogue of the Freedmen (Cyrenians, Alexandrians, and those from Cilicia and Asia).** To flash back to the Hellenistic group mentioned in Acts 2, it is conceivable that Parthian-Hellenists, Egyptian-Hellenists, Mesopotamian-Hellenists, Arab-Hellenists and many others would prefer the close fellowship of their own ethnic-oriented synagogues.

We are not sure, but it could well be that by this time the born-again Hellenists outnumbered the Hebrew followers of Jesus in the Jerusalem church.

Who Is Running the Church?

Here we have a phenomenon very common in cross-cultural ministries today. The church is bicultural, Hebrews and Hellenists, but only one of the groups, the Hebrews, is providing the top leadership. The apostles were all Hebrews. Like many missionaries today, who have fallen into the error of assuming the leadership of churches in the new cultures to which they have been called, the apostles were probably talking behind the Hellenist believers' backs in Aramaic, a language the Hellenists could not understand. No wonder friction developed!

Some may question why such a conflict would occur, considering that the Hebrews were natives of Palestine. They were not foreign missionaries. This raises the extremely crucial missiological issue of the distinction between *cultural* differences and *geographical* differences among people groups. Cross-cultural (E-2 and E-3) evangelistic challenges can be found in the same city as well as in the same neighborhood. Often those who are born in the same country and live in close proximity to unreached people groups would not be the most likely to evangelize them. A rather sad case in point is that Anglo-Americans are not a very likely force for evangelism to unreached American Indian tribes even though the members of both groups are natives of the United States. The relationship of Hebrews to Hellenists is a missiological issue even though the Hebrews did not travel out-side their native land to become involved.

One of the most crucial issues in cross-cultural missions is leadership selection and training. We are soon going to see that when the apostle Paul planted new churches among the Gentiles he almost immediately ordained leaders in the churches, leaders who understood the language, ate the same food, shared common values and handled money in mutually acceptable ways.

The way the Hebrews were handling the money in the Jerusalem church was not acceptable to their Hellenist brothers and sisters, and a serious dispute arose as a result.

The Widow Problem (Acts 6:1)

1. ...there arose a murmuring against the Hebrews by the Hellenists, because their widows were neglected in the daily distribution.

As I have mentioned, the problem concerning widows was only a symptom of a much deeper issue revolving around cultural dissonance. Multiethnic situations, where people programmed with different sets of cultural values and behavior patterns are forced to live in close proximity to each other, are inherently loaded with potential areas of conflict. As we well know in our modern multicultural United States society, these areas most frequently involve perceived issues of injustice, discrimination, unfairness, prejudice and oppression. Usually the minority group realizes what is happening long before the majority group.

At this point, as I have said, the numerical majority of the Jerusalem church might have been Hellenists. But in issues of social justice, the determining factor is not necessarily numbers, but *power,* as black South Africans, who are the vast numerical majority in their nation, have long realized. In Jerusalem, the church leaders were Hebrews and they had the power. This put the Hellenists in a minority position despite their numbers.

Why the Hellenists Were Upset

Why, then, would care for widows become an issue of justice in the eyes of the Hellenists? Let's look at it.

First of all, most of the widows who needed help were undoubtedly Hellenists. For a starter, the Hellenists had a much higher age profile than the Hebrews because, as has been mentioned, the more elderly, retired Hellenists from all over the Jewish dispersion were the ones moving back to Jerusalem to live out their days in the holy city. For many, this move would involve a physical separation from their extended families who still lived out there in Asia or Rome or Alexandria or wherever. Jews ordinarily have tight family ties, so when a Hebrew father would die, his widow would more than likely be cared for by her grown children who lived there in Jerusalem or nearby. But not the Hellenistic widow because her grown children were not in Jerusalem. It, consequently, became the responsibility of the church to see that she was cared for.

Second, it would be reasonable to suspect that most of the money in the Jerusalem church benevolence fund would be Hellenistic money. Because they were rich enough to retire in Jerusalem, most Hellenists would probably be upper-middle to upper class. It could well be that the Hebrews would tend to be drawn from the middle to lower-middle classes in Jerusalem. In fact, after the Hellenists left Jerusalem later on, the Jerusalem church became known for its poverty (see Rom. 15:26). If this is true, a good bit of the property that had been sold and donated to the church would presumably be Hellenists' property.

Third, the major complication has to do with the leadership. If my assumptions are valid, although most widows were Hellenists and most of the money was Hellenist money, the leadership who had the power to determine how the money was spent were Hebrews, namely the 12 apostles. This, understandably, irritated the Hellenists.

None of this is to imply that the apostles were not wonderful people, filled with the Holy Spirit, exhibiting the fruit of the Spirit in their daily lives and thinking that they were treating the Hellenists with fairness and deep Christian compassion. Their character was not the problem. The problem was that they were monocultural and were just beginning to learn how to relate to brothers and sisters in Christ from a different culture. Their *spirituality* was not deficient, their *missiology* was.

One of the most difficult lessons for cross-cultural missionaries to learn is that when they plant a church in a culture different from their own, the leadership of the new church must come from those rooted in the second culture or the new church will not grow and develop as it should. Missionaries frequently assume that because they have been Christians longer and know the Bible better and pray more and adhere more rigidly to norms of Christian behavior that they can, and should, assume leadership of the new church. They do so, however, to their own detriment and hinder the spread of the gospel over the long haul. I say long haul, because naturally some leadership must be given by the missionaries to the initial nucleus of babes in Christ who still need the milk of the Word. But the sooner this is turned over to the nationals the better.

This is the missiological lesson God was teaching the apostles in Jerusalem through what was, undoubtedly, for them a painful experience. They assumed, as do many missionaries, that those from the second culture could become part of their church and peacefully accept their leadership. Such things do happen, but they are the exceptions, not the rule. A familiar example of an exception to the rule would be slaves in the Deep South in the days of Uncle Tom, many of whom became faithful Christians, but who were forced to join churches led by whites and made to sit together in the balcony. Such an arrangement, however, is not the best pattern for the long haul in attempting to win the lost in a multicultural society.

The Conflict Erupts!

This problem involving a social injustice toward a minority in the church, similar to a volcano, may have appeared dormant for a time, but eventually the top blew off and it erupted. The Hellenists became so irritated that they rose up. In such situations today, they might have said, "Missionary, go home!" In many ways, the Hellenists' **murmuring against the Hebrews** was a functional equivalent.

So the Hellenists complained. Somehow their grievances, which presumably up to that time had been talked of only behind closed doors in their Messianic synagogues and home groups, came to the surface. As is often the case, the apostles could have been among the last to know that they had a severe problem on their hands. They had been very busy in giving leadership to the rapidly growing church, they were elated at continual reports of healings and miracles and they thought everything was all right. But, obviously, things were going wrong, so they had to take some action.

Conflict Resolution

....

2. Then the twelve summoned the multitude of the disciples...

....

To begin the process of conflict resolution, the apostles wisely called a congregational meeting. This action in itself indicates that by then they had realized the problem was serious. Such a meeting of **the multitude of disciples** would not be called again, to our knowledge. When another conflict arose later on in Acts 15, it would be resolved by a council of leaders instead.

We have no reason to imagine that all 25,000 believers, if indeed that many were in the city, would attend this meeting. If our contemporary experience is any indication, most church members are not particularly anxious to go to a business meeting. I would imagine that those who were motivated to attend would largely be Hellenists because they were the ones who brought the grievance. So the nature of the gathering would most likely be the Hebrew apostles meeting with the Hellenist disciples to listen to their point of view and to gather the facts necessary to make the decision.

We also need to realize that this meeting would not have been organized and run under Roberts' Rules of Order, as a typical United States congregational meeting might be run today. The church government was not based on taking votes with the majority winning. God had given the spiritual authority to the 12 apostles, and the final decision would be theirs. However, they desired to base their decision on accurate information and an accurate reading of the emotional state of affairs of the believers. I can imagine that a meeting of this nature would not have been dull or boring.

The Apostles' Position

....

2. Then the twelve summoned the multitude of the disciples and said, "It is not desirable that we should leave the word of God and serve tables. 4. but we will give

> ourselves continually to prayer and to the
> ministry of the word."

After carefully considering the matter, the apostles were ready to announce their decision. First they wanted to make their own position clear to the church. They had decided that from now on they would give their full time to the *spiritual* leadership of the church and leave *administrative* matters to others.

Among other things, the apostles by then were probably beginning to come to terms with their spiritual gifts. It takes time to know with reasonable assurance what our spiritual gifts are, but when we do know, God expects us to build our ministry schedules around them. The apostles were learning that they did not have the ability or the gifts to manage a multicultural church and handle the problems of the Hellenists competently. I would imagine that, as frequently happens on the mission field today, a number of serious issues were hidden under the surface, and the widow problem was simply the one that first became public.

I realize many do not like to imagine that great spiritual leaders such as the 12 apostles were unable to rise above cultural limitations. Therefore, they like to think of this incident as simply a matter of efficient church administration rather than as an ethnic clash. But if any would doubt that the apostles were still ethnocentric, the doubts will go away when we later see how they dealt with Peter when he came back from the house of Cornelius in Acts 10, and with Paul when he finished his first term of missionary service among Gentiles in Acts 15.

Fortunately, the apostles were flexible. They were learning how to relate to those of a different culture. By this time, it had become clear to them that the Hellenist segment of the church needed Hellenistic leadership. Although they might well have been in a state of denial previously, the reality was dawning on them, as Howard Marshall says, "that the Aramaic-Speaking Christians and the Greek-Speaking Christians were dividing into two separate groups."[6]

As we find out later in Acts, this division was not a small one or a temporary one. The great persecution that followed Stephen's ministry drove out from Jerusalem the *Hellenists* but not the *Hebrews*, according to the implications of Acts 8:1. Of that event, Ernst Haenchen says, "At the moment of the persecution the primitive community embodied two groups which were already so clearly distinct even to outsiders that the one was persecuted, the other left unharmed."[7]

Selecting the New Leaders

3. Therefore, brethren, seek out from among you seven men of good reputation, full of the Holy Spirit and wisdom, whom we may appoint over this business;
5. And the saying pleased the whole multitude....

The verb for leadership selection, **seek out**, is translated in other versions as "choose" or "select," or words to that effect. Many of us have a tendency to read our own culture back into the text and imagine that they must have held an election. I do not believe this was the case. The seven did not become leaders as a result of either an election or the apostles' whim, but they had already emerged as leaders and had been so recognized among their own people group long before.

We do not create leaders in the church by choosing them. God has already created them and chosen them and given them appropriate gifts, and they are thus recognized by all as leaders when the church is healthy. Elections, campaigning and rivalry among candidates for leadership has no place in the church. Acts mentions no elections after the coming of the Spirit on the Day of Pentecost!

These leaders were to be chosen **from among you.** Among whom? A corollary of the cultural distinctions within the Jerusalem church, which I have been detailing, would be that they would be chosen by the Hellenists from among the Hellenists. Missiologists call this "indigenizing the church." The indigenous church is a church that governs itself, finances itself and propagates itself. The essential first step toward making this happen is to choose leaders from among them who are culturally compatible and who will be sensitive to special needs of the church members, such as caring for widows in this case.

Although the cultural match is a beginning, the leaders must also be **of good reputation.** Presumably, they will be high-visibility individuals whose lives have been openly scrutinized by believers and nonbelievers alike. They need to be people of high moral and ethical standards and respected as such by the community.

Only those **full of the Holy Spirit** should be considered for top church leadership. This is an interesting qualification because it clearly implies that not all Christians are, in fact, full of the Holy Spirit. This, obviously, is not a statement dealing with the *presence* of the Holy Spirit in the believer, because He is present in all. Paul says, "Do you not know that your body is the temple of the Holy Spirit who is in you?" (1 Cor. 6:19). So if the people were to choose only those **full of the Holy Spirit,** how could they tell which ones were?

For one thing, they could look for those who had exhibited in their lives the *fruit* of the Holy Spirit: "love, joy, peace, longsuffering, kindness, goodness, faithfulness, gentleness, self-control," according to Galatians 5:22,23. These qualities would also have contributed to making them people **of good reputation.**

For another thing, they could have observed the ones through whom the miraculous work of the Holy Spirit was already being done in power ministries, and it appears they did so. Later, we are told that Stephen **did great wonders and signs among the people** (Acts 6:8), and that Philip did many miracles (see Acts 8:6,7).

The new leaders should be those **full of wisdom.** They were to be practical people who could make good decisions.

The apostles themselves modeled the kind of wisdom and good decision making they recommended to others. Therefore, **the saying pleased the whole multitude.** When leadership is anointed by God, their decisions are readily accepted by the people. The vision and initiative comes from the leadership, but it meets the needs of the group and is pleasing to all. This is what is implied in the biblical concept of "servant leadership." People follow servant leaders because they are confident that the decisions made will be decisions for the benefit of the followers. Good leaders have a reputation of not making decisions for personal benefit. In this case, the apostles were relinquishing a great deal of power for the benefit of the church as a whole. Not only would they end up with fewer people under their direct authority, but they also were giving up control of considerable financial resources that in themselves were a significant source of power.

Who Were the Leaders?

....

5. ...And they chose Stephen, a man full of faith and the
Holy Spirit, and Philip, Prochorus, Nicanor, Timon,
Parmenas, and Nicolas, a proselyte from Antioch,
6. whom they set before the apostles; and when
they had prayed, they laid hands on them.

....

Knowing what we now know, it comes as no surprise that the seven leaders chosen by the Hellenists were all themselves

Hellenists. How do we know they were? We know by the names, all being Greek names. Some Bible scholars do not think it would have been a proper thing for the Jerusalem church that they should all be Hellenists, so they argue that in those days there was no prohibition on Hebrews taking Greek names. However, I agree with Hans Conzelmann, who says, "It is true that even in Palestine, Greek names are common (cf. Andrew and Philip from the circle of the Twelve), but still it is remarkable that in an entire group not a single non-Greek appears."[8] In his more recent commentary, Simon Kistemaker reports the consensus that "scholars favor the explanation that all seven were Hellenistic Jews whose native tongue was Greek."[9]

Three of them, Nicanor, Timon and Parmenas are relatively unknown. Nicolas is the only one of the seven not born an ethnic Jew. He was a proselyte, which means he was born a Gentile and chose to become a Jew. So he was a Jew by adoption, not by birth, so to speak. Prochorus later becomes a bishop, according to history. The two most prominent among the seven were Philip and Stephen.

Philip is not to be confused with Philip of Bethsaida whom Jesus early on called by saying, "Follow Me," and who then brought Nathanael to Jesus, both becoming part of the 12 disciples (see John 1:43-45). That Philip was a Galilean Aramaic-speaking Hebrew, a member of Jesus' own ethnic group. This Philip, a Greek-speaking Hellenistic Jew, later became known as **Philip the evangelist** (Acts 21:8) and he is the pioneer missionary to the Samaritans in Acts 8.

Stephen is clearly the most prominent member of the seven. In fact, Luke takes pains to pause right in the roll call to record that Stephen was **a man full of faith and the Holy Spirit**. This is quite a compliment, which Luke later uses once again to describe Barnabas in Acts 11:24. The faith that characterized

Stephen, apparently, was more than the saving faith each Christian must have, and more than the faith that is the expected fruit of the Spirit, but probably it was the spiritual gift of faith mentioned in 1 Corinthians 12:9. This is the faith to "remove mountains," as Paul says in 1 Corinthians 13:2. The rest of Acts 6 and all of Acts 7 tell the glorious, and yet sad, story of how Stephen became Christianity's most famous martyr.

Were the Seven Hellenists "Deacons"?

Many sermons I have heard on Acts 6 regard the seven as the first local church board of deacons, and make their applications to the office of deacon that has been established in many churches today. One reason they do this is because most of the commentaries preachers would likely consult give this interpretation. The assumption is that the 12 apostles delegated their day-to-day administrative chores to these seven so they could distribute food while the apostles did the important things, such as praying and teaching the Word. Their main function, in this view, was to relieve the top leadership of busywork. *The New Testament in Modern English*, by Philips, has a subtitle over this passage: "The first deacons are chosen."

My own view, as I have been explaining, is quite different. I agree with Derek Tidball who points out that the seven "are not subsequently seen as table-waiters but as preachers and missionaries. Some scholars have therefore concluded that they did not form a group beneath the apostles, but alongside of them—a distinct ethnic leadership group."[10] Although Luke is gentle in the way he records this historical event, its significance for missiology and the advance of the Kingdom into Samaria and the end of the earth is enormous. These are definitely more than your run-of-the-mill "deacons."

The Greek word behind "deacon" is *diakonia*, which in today's

English means ministry or service. Here is how John Stott explains it: "*Diakonia* is a generic word for service; it lacks specificity until a descriptive adjective is added, whether 'pastoral,' 'social,' 'political,' 'medical,' or another. All Christians without exception...are themselves called to ministry."[11] In this sense, therefore, it would not be inaccurate to say the seven were "deacons," although the word itself, *diakonos*, is not used at all in the passage.

However, this leads us nowhere because other forms related to the word *diakonos* are used here both for the ministry to **serve tables** (6:2), commonly attributed to the seven, and also **ministry of the word** (6:4), commonly attributed to the 12. If the 7 were "deacons," then the 12 apostles were "deacons" also, as far as the Greek text is concerned.

If the seven were deacons appointed to do social work among the entire conglomerate Jerusalem church, it would then make little sense for them all to be Hellenists. That is why, as I mentioned before, several commentators attempt to argue that the seven must have included some Hebrews who used Greek names. Why would some take pains to argue that the seven were essentially table-servers when the facts seem to point in such a different direction? Unless I am mistaken, it is primarily because these commentators are extremely uncomfortable with the thought that two ethnic groups in the same church could not get along with each other. It does not seem politically correct to them when sociologist Derek Tidball says, "The strong coherence of the small band of Jesus' disciples was therefore now broken."[12] However, it is a fact that must be recognized, and a further indication that, as Hans Conzelmann says, the seven "do not stand *beneath* the Twelve, but *alongside* them."[13]

The Positive Outcome of Church Division

Although the term is harsher than Luke would use, this passage is an account of the first major church split. We often think of church splits in a negative light because so many we have seen or heard of are ugly, carnal affairs. They need not be that way, however, as we learn from the Jerusalem church. This was done by the leading of the Holy Spirit for the best of both parties and for the glory of God. What happened?

> **7. And the word of God spread, and the number of the disciples multiplied greatly in Jerusalem, and a great many of the priests were obedient to the faith.**

Whenever Luke gives such an upbeat report of church growth in Acts, it is because the outcome of what has just happened, even if it is something like the apostles' being physically beaten by the Sanhedrin (see Acts 5:40-42), has a positive outcome for the kingdom of God. The outcome of this case of church division was no exception.

The Hellenist believers immediately became content and stopped their murmuring. They were no longer under the leadership of Aramaic-speaking Hebrews who had hillbilly roots in Galilee. Their new leaders were, from their perspective, cosmopolitan, well educated, affluent and spiritual Christians who could easily understand their problem not only with widows but also anything else that would arise. They now felt liberated and, therefore, could be more enthusiastic about serving God and extending His kingdom.

For the first time in this rapid spread of the gospel, **a great many of the priests were obedient to the faith.** This raises the interesting question: Why did the movement of the Gospel among the priests begin only after the Jerusalem church had undergone its ethnic division? Let's look at it.

These priests are not to be confused with the high priests who joined the Sadducees in persecuting the apostles (see Acts 4:1 and 5:17). Joachim Jeremias calculates, rather laboriously, the number of priests in Jerusalem to be approximately 8,000 along with some 10,000 Levites.[14] Ernst Haenchen affirms that, "The eight thousand or so priests had livings so exiguous that they were obliged to follow a trade during the ten or eleven months in which their service of the Temple left them free to do so."[15] Richard Rackham adds, "There was a great gulf between the ordinary priests and the class of ruling and wealthy 'high priests.'"[16]

These priests were poor, while the high priests and the Sadducees were rich and would have had a great deal to lose from the change in the political status quo that the Jesus movement was threatening. But the ordinary priests would have had nothing to lose and everything to gain by following Jesus as Messiah. There is some evidence, in fact, that they were being exploited by the high priests. Because of this, Rackham's conclusion sounds very plausible: "So when a large body of the priests joined the apostles, it would have the effect, politically, of a very practical protest against their Sadducean rulers."[17]

If this is correct, why would the priests have waited so long to commit themselves to the new faith? My hypothesis, and it is only that, is that the priests would have been extremely ethnocentric Hebrews. As long as the church was perceived by them, as outsiders, to be a mixture of Hebrews along with the Hellenists, the priests would not want to consider responding to the gospel they were preaching. But when the Hellenists became indigenized and moved out under their own leadership, the priests now could become a part of a more purely Hebrew Messianic community without compromising their own integrity. This was still a Messianic Jewish (not a "Christian") group, and the priests would naturally have continued performing their Temple duties as always.

The principle is that the multiplication of many different kinds of churches, including those along ethnic lines, provides more options for unbelievers who are looking for a church in which they think they can feel comfortable. When this opportunity is available, their decision for Christ is properly a religious, rather than a social or cultural, decision. The result is, as Luke indicates, that **the disciples multiplied greatly** and churches grow.

Positioning for the Future

The most important outcome of this landmark event, in my opinion, was the learning experience it provided for the leaders of the Jerusalem church, which they would later apply to taking the gospel of Christ past Jerusalem and Judea out to Samaria and the end of the earth. The 12 apostles received a crash course in missiology. Although they did not all become cross-cultural missionaries, they were finally poised to provide what leadership they could to a new era of international evangelism. The first major step in that direction would be taken by Stephen, one of the Hellenist leaders they had just laid hands on and blessed.

Reflection Questions

1. The chief players in the unfolding of Acts 6 are Hebrew Jews as opposed to Hellenistic Jews. Discuss the differing characteristics of each group.
2. When two strong ethnic groups are in the same church, conflict frequently surfaces. In this case, the problem centered on widows. What was it about widows that upset the Hellenists?
3. When missionaries plant a church and then insist on retaining the leadership for too long a time, they frequently run into

serious trouble. Did the Hebrew apostles in Jerusalem make a similar mistake?

4. It is common to regard the seven individuals whom the apostles chose as "deacons." Were they deacons as we understand the word today, or were they something else?

5. Can anything good come out of a church split? Explain your response.

Notes

1. R. C. H. Lenski, *The Interpretation of The Acts of the Apostles* (Minneapolis, MN: Augsburg Publishing House, 1934), p. 239.

2. Donald A. McGavran, *Understanding Church Growth* (Grand Rapids, MI: William B. Eerdmans Publishing Co., 1990), p. 67. Used by permission.

3. I. Howard Marshall, *The Acts of the Apostles* (Leicester, England, Inter-Varsity Press, 1980), p. 125. Used by permission.

4. Simon J. Kistemaker, *New Testament Commentary: Exposition on the Acts of the Apostles* (Grand Rapids, MI: Baker Book House Company, 1990), p. 220. Used by permission.

5. Ibid.

6. Marshall, *Acts*, p. 125.

7. Ernst Haenchen, *The Acts of the Apostles: A Commentary* (Louisville, KY: The Westminster Press, 1971), p. 266.

8. Hans Conzelmann, *History of Primitive Christianity* (Nashville, TN: Abingdon Press, 1973), p. 57.

9. Kistemaker, *Exposition*, p. 224.

10. Derek Tidball, *The Social Context of the New Testament* (Grand Rapids, MI: Academie Books, Zondervan Publishing House, 1984), p. 55.

11. John Stott, *The Spirit, the World and the Church* (Downers Grove, IL: InterVarsity Press, 1990), p. 122.

12. Tidball, *The Social Context*, p. 55.

13. Conzelmann, *History*, p. 58.

14. Reprinted from *Jerusalem in the Time of Jesus* by Joachim Jeremias, copyright © 1969 SCM. Used by permission of Augsburg Fortress (p. 204).

15. Haenchen, *Acts*, p. 264.

16. Richard Belward Rackham, *The Acts of the Apostles: An Exposition* (London, England, Methuen & Co. Ltd., 1901), p. 87.
17. Ibid.

CHAPTER

8

Acts 6, 7 and 8

Samaria: Preaching on the Other Side of the Tracks

Acts 6, 7 and 8

Up to this point, we have been dealing with E-1 and E-2 evangelism. As a reminder, E-1 is monocultural evangelism, reaching people from the same culture. Our example was Hebrew Jews evangelizing Hebrew Jews whether they happened to be Galilean Hebrews or Judean Hebrews. E-2 is cross-cultural evangelism, but across a relatively narrow cultural barrier, such as Hebrew Jews evangelizing Hellenistic Jews.

Now we move on to E-3 evangelism, taking the gospel to Samaria. The cross-cultural barrier here is much higher. As we saw in the last chapter, Hebrews and Hellenists had enough of a challenge getting along with each other, but that was minor compared to the challenge of reaching the much-despised Samaritans for Christ.

Jesus' Great Commission in Acts 1:8 was: **"You shall receive** power when the Holy Spirit has come upon you; and you shall be witnesses to Me in Jerusalem, and in all Judea and Samaria, and to the end of the earth." The top leader for advancing the Kingdom in Jerusalem and Judea was Peter. The two leaders for moving into Samaria are now Stephen and Philip, and the leader for the Gentiles will be Paul. These are the four chief figures in the whole book of Acts.

Many get so caught up with the drama of Stephen's execution that they fail to see clearly how Stephen's ministry prepared the way for Philip's evangelistic mission in Samaria. Actually, as I will explain in considerable detail, Stephen was the *theoretician* for this first bold E-3 initiative, while Philip was the *practitioner* who implemented the theory.

When I say "bold" initiative, the implications of Jews showing love to Samaritans and sharing their faith with them was so radical in the eyes of unbelieving Jews that not only did they execute Stephen for suggesting it, but they also drove most of Stephen's fellow Hellenistic disciples out of the city of Jerusalem.

The crucial question we will first deal with is: Why was Stephen executed? Understanding this will clear up other questions we might have about basic mechanisms underlying cross-cultural missions in general.

Stephen and His Ministry
Acts 6

....

8. And Stephen, full of faith and power, did great wonders and signs among the people. 10. And they were not able to resist the wisdom and the Spirit by which he spoke.

....

As we detailed in the last chapter, Stephen was much more than a "deacon" or a social worker running errands for the 12 apostles.

He was a strong leader in his own right and had earned his leadership status among the Hellenists long before the apostles laid hands on him. Despite the brevity of his ministry, Stephen is unquestionably one of the most important figures in the history of the Christian movement.

Among other things, Stephen **did great wonders and signs among the people.** This is of more than passing interest because it is the first time in the book of Acts that Luke attributes ministry in the miraculous to anyone but the 12 apostles. This is another way of Luke's informing us that Stephen, and by implication the other six Hellenistic leaders, ranked not *under* the apostles, but *alongside* them. These signs and wonders drew widespread attention to Stephen's message of salvation and large numbers were responding.

At this point, some raise the question about whether believers in general should expect to participate in power ministries by healing the sick and casting out demons, or whether this is restricted to the apostles and those upon whom the apostles personally laid hands, such as Stephen. Some theologians, such as the renowned Benjamin Breckinridge Warfield of Princeton Theological Seminary in the early years of our century, have made a doctrinal position out of this issue called "cessationism." They argue that miraculous works, such as healings and miracles and prophecy, ceased when those such as Stephen passed from the scene, and works of supernatural power were no longer a part of the normal ministry of the Church from then on.

Fortunately, in my view, this position is steadily becoming extinct. Jack Deere's recent book, *Surprised by the Power of the Spirit* (Zondervan), has discredited cessationism almost to the point of a coup de grâce. Nevertheless, you will still find in some standard commentaries statements affirming that we must not imagine that Stephen ministered in areas of power and the miraculous before the apostles laid on their hands. If he had, it would tend to discredit their cessationist theory.

I agree with F. F. Bruce, who says, "Since at that time [Stephen] was already 'full of faith and the Holy Spirit' (v. 5), it is reasonable to conclude that this fullness was accompanied by the 'grace and power' which enabled him to perform ['great signs and wonders']."[1] When we think of it, in the environment of what we know of the Jerusalem church, quite possibly no one would have ever been considered for top leadership among the Hebrews or the Hellenists who was not already being used by God in power ministries. That is why the apostles set forth as one of the leadership qualifications **full of the Holy Spirit** (Acts 6:3).

Although I believe and teach that all committed disciples of Jesus Christ should expect to heal the sick and cast out demons by the power of the Holy Spirit (see John 14:12), I also realize that not all will minister with the same degree of power. Stephen was one of those who saw more dramatic results from his ministry than others. It is not Luke's ongoing custom to use adjectives to describe the quality of signs and wonders, but here is an exception. He says that Stephen's were **great.**

Luke also mentions that Stephen's opponents **were not able to resist the wisdom and the Spirit by which he spoke.** Stephen ministered in word and deed. His deeds were the miracles, and his word was the spoken message of the death and resurrection of Jesus Christ. Stephen's message was so reasonable and he could defend it so well that he won all the arguments. Because his enemies found they could not silence him intellectually, they decided to take their only viable recourse and silence him physically.

The False Accusation

9. Then there arose some from what is called the

Synagogue of the Freedmen...disputing with Stephen.
11. Then they secretly induced men to say, "We
have heard him speak blasphemous words against
Moses and God." 12. And they stirred up the
people, the elders, and the scribes; and they came upon
him, seized him, and brought him to the council.
13. They also set up false witnesses who said,
"This man does not cease to speak blasphemous
words against this holy place and the law;
14. for we have heard him say that this Jesus
of Nazareth will destroy this place and change
the customs which Moses delivered to us."

Somewhat predictably, the enemies of Stephen, who was a Hellenist, would emerge from among the unbelieving Hellenistic Jews who worshiped in the various synagogues in Jerusalem, such as the Synagogue of the Freedmen. Once the Hellenistic church had been indigenized and secured its own leadership, it began growing even more rapidly and, therefore, posed an increasingly serious threat to the status quo of the Hellenistic community in general. The previous opposition, when only the Hebrew apostles were leading, came from the Hebrew Sadducees. Of course, even in this case, it eventually got back to the council, which was the Sanhedrin with its majority of Sadducees, but that is not where it began.

Why would the Hellenists, who did not seem to be as rigid in applying the strict Jewish lifestyle as the Hebrews, become so upset over Stephen? My guess is that there might be two reasons: one emotional and one theological.

As is frequently the case, the emotional reason precedes the theological reason. First-century Jerusalem, as I have said, was similar to Miami Beach, a wonderful place for Jews to retire and live out their days. A high value in retirement communities is peace and predictability. The Hellenists, as a group, would have invested a considerable amount of money in Jerusalem with the goal of creating and maintaining a high quality of life. They were very proud of their city the way it was, and threats to its social stability were not necessarily welcomed.

If the picture we have of the explosion of the Messianic Jewish movement throughout the city of Jerusalem is anywhere near accurate, a major social disruption was going on. The lame were walking, the blind were seeing, the dead were being raised and people were speaking in languages they had never learned. It was bad enough when this movement was being led by motley, rustic Galileans, but even worse when led by sophisticated Hellenists such as Stephen. Leisure World in Zion was experiencing a spiritual earthquake, and collective emotions were definitely on edge. Something had to be done to stop it! The basic well-being of the Hellenists was severely threatened!

The Hellenistic Jews knew that they could not build a strong enough case against Stephen on social or emotional grounds alone. They, therefore, began to search Stephen's teaching for possible theological flaws, particularly because blasphemy was a serious crime in Jerusalem. Therefore, the accusation, false as it was, took on two parts: (1) **We have heard him speak blasphemous words against Moses,** and (2) **This man does not cease to speak blasphemous words against this holy place,** meaning the Temple.

These were very serious accusations, and in each they attempted to implicate *both* Stephen and Jesus of Nazareth:

- Stephen speaks against Moses and the law (6:11,13),

and Jesus wants to change the customs of
Moses (6:14)
- Stephen speaks against God and His Temple
(6:11,13), and Jesus wants to destroy the
Temple (6:14).

The Real Issue

Because neither of the above charges was true, there must be a
more fundamental underlying problem. What was it? Let's first
attempt to understand the Jewish point of view, then Stephen's
point of view.

The Jewish Point of View

God is a tribal God, the God of Israel, His chosen people. Other
people groups have their gods as well, but the God of Israel is the
one true God. Jehovah was *only* the God of Israel, not of other
peoples. This was a religious concept, but also a patriotic one.
The whole internal fabric of the nation of Israel would stand or
fall on that doctrine of God.

Access to God could only be attained through the priests in
Jerusalem and the sacrifices in the Jewish Temple. Multiple synagogues were not *substitutes* for the Temple, only *reflections* of it.
Because the Temple was so crucial, hundreds of thousands of Jews
from the dispersion would return to Jerusalem for the various
feast days each year to gain access to God. In no other place
could He be found in that way.

God would welcome non-Jews from other peoples of the
world. But they could not access God in their own people groups
because Jehovah was only the God of Israel, not of their peoples.
If they wanted to worship Jehovah God, they would first need to
repudiate their native cultural ties and consent to become Jewish
through prescribed rites such as baptism and circumcision. At the

time, the Jews were sending out proselytizing bands to evangelize other people groups and encourage Gentiles to become Jews and, thus, to find God. Once they did, the mutual understanding was that they were no longer Gentiles, but Jews. One of the seven new Hellenistic leaders, Nicolas, was a former Gentile who had done this (see Acts 6:5), and they were called Jewish proselytes.

Stephen's Point of View

Under the anointing of the Holy Spirit, Stephen had realized that Jehovah God was sovereign over the whole universe. He was the God not only of Israel, but also the God of every nation on earth. Stephen might have remembered the psalm that says, "The Lord is great in Zion, and He is high above *all the peoples*" (Ps. 99:2).

The Jewish symbols of God's presence—the Temple and the law of Moses—were true and valid. Stephen would never have spoken against the Jews' obeying the law and accessing God in the Temple. He himself obeyed the law and worshiped in the Temple. The accusations were so absurd that Stephen's enemies had to find false witnesses.

Stephen also knew that although the Temple and the law were *valid*, they were not *exclusive* means of finding God. Here is his main difference with the unbelieving Jews: Stephen was implying that people do not have to become Jews in order to get to God! Stephen at some time may have quoted Jesus' words to the Samaritan woman: "The hour is coming when you will neither on this mountain, nor in Jerusalem, worship the Father....God is Spirit, and those who worship Him must worship in spirit and truth" (John 4:21,24).

Although the gospel was being preached in Jerusalem and Judea, it was being preached to Jews only and this had not become an issue. Stephen has now gone down in history as one of Christianity's greatest leaders because he was the first one who began to prepare the way for the gospel to move out of the Jewish sphere and to the Samaritans and the Gentiles. The gospel was for *panta ta ethne, all* the peoples, and not just the Jews (see Acts 7:48-50). As we will see below, this was Stephen's point of view and this is what severely threatened his enemies and made them angry. They were not willing to share their God!

Stephen's Landmark Speech

Stephen's response to these false accusations is the longest speech recorded in the book of Acts. Why? Unquestionably, it is Scripture's most important missiological statement other than the findings of the Council of Jerusalem in Acts 15. It is not a mere coincidence that they both deal with exactly the same issue. What is the issue? Simply put, here it is: *It is not necessary to give up your own culture and to become a Jew (or anything else for that matter) in order to be saved.*

Stephen had a special anointing of God for delivering this speech:

....

15. And all who sat in the council, looking steadfastly at him, saw his face as the face of an angel.

....

This anointing enabled Stephen to do two things that someone in his position ordinarily would not be expected to do. First, he did not deal with negatives by accusing the accusers of giving false testimony. He dealt only with positives. Second, he accused the leaders so forcefully of murdering Jesus that they never even let him finish his discourse.

How God Spoke to His People: Acts 7

2. And he said, "Men and brethren and fathers, listen: The God of glory appeared to our father Abraham when he was in Mesopotamia,... 9. And the patriarchs, becoming envious, sold Joseph into Egypt. But God was with him 30. And when forty years had passed, an Angel of the Lord appeared to him [Moses] in a flame of fire in a bush, in the wilderness of Mount Sinai. 44. Our fathers had the tabernacle of witness in the wilderness,..."

In order to make his point, Stephen chooses three of the outstanding heroes of the Jewish faith: Abraham, Joseph and Moses. No Jew would doubt that God had spoken to each of them personally, but He spoke to all of them *outside* of the Holy Land. He spoke to Moses in Mesopotamia, to Joseph in Egypt and to Moses on Mount Sinai. The implication: None of them needed to come to the Temple in Jerusalem to hear from God!

Then Stephen refers to the portable tabernacle in the wilderness, which also was outside the Holy Land, that could be used any place to bring people into contact with God. He goes on to contrast this to the Temple:

47. "But Solomon built Him a house. 48. However, the Most High does not dwell in temples made with hands,..."

In all probability, not one of the 12 apostles, at this point, could have so clearly expounded the doctrine that the gospel of the Kingdom is much broader than Judaism with its symbols and rituals. Being a Hellenist would have helped Stephen immensely to comprehend this insight and draw out its missiological implications. The Hebrew believers had not yet really accepted it when Peter later went to the house of Cornelius (see Acts 10) and when the Jerusalem Council was convened almost 20 years later (see Acts 15). Some, in fact, never did catch on.

Applying the Principle to Samaria

The general principle behind Stephen's speech is that God's people *must* move out in mission. They must become, to use the title of Charles Van Engen's excellent book, *God's Missionary People*. Van Engen says, "As local congregations are built up to reach out, they will emerge from their sapling stage to be their true nature, bearing fruit as missionary people."[2]

It may well be that even as he was speaking to the Sanhedrin, Stephen knew that the time had come to preach in Samaria. Scholars point to two indirect references to Samaria in his speech that could have been intentional, but that the average reader might not notice. Stephen speaks of the tomb in Shechem **that Abraham bought** (7:16). That tomb was located in Samaria. Also, from Deuteronomy, he cites the promise of a prophet to come (see Acts 7:37), which was the only Messianic prophecy the Samaritans had accepted. How would Stephen have known? Because he was filled with the Holy Spirit, it may well have been a prophetic word from God.

Who were these Samaritans?

After the time of King Solomon, the northern Israelite kingdom called "Israel," separated from the southern Israelite kingdom called "Judah." The capital city of the northern kingdom was Samaria and sometimes, therefore, the whole northern kingdom is referred to as "Samaria," after the city. In 721 B.C., the neighboring Assyrians captured Samaria and forced the Israelites there to intermarry with them, creating a mixed Israelite-Assyrian race. From that time on, they were considered impure and non-Jewish by the pure-blooded Jews. The Samaritans offered to help build the Temple in Jerusalem, but were turned down, so they built their own temple at Mount Gerazim, which the Jews later proceeded to destroy. Samaritans and Jews disliked each other immensely. The woman at the well reflected this when she casually said to Jesus, "How is that You, being a Jew, ask a drink from me, a Samaritan woman?" (John 4:9).

Stephen knew this, of course, and he, therefore, knew that the Samaritans would never accept worship at the Jewish Temple in Jerusalem as a precondition for salvation through Jesus as Messiah. Therefore, in order to contextualize the gospel for Samaritans, Stephen had to deabsolutize Jewish temple worship as the one and only way to come to Jehovah God. Nothing was wrong with the temple—Stephen himself worshiped there—but cross-culturally it was excess baggage if loaded onto the simple gospel of repentance for sin and faith in Jesus Christ. To the Sanhedrin, such a thing would sound like blasphemy.

As if that weren't bad enough, Stephen went on to accuse his accusers, not of giving false testimony, but more ominously of murdering their Messiah:

....

51. "You stiffnecked and uncircumcised in heart and ears!
You always resist the Holy Spirit; as your fathers did,
so do you. 52. Which of the prophets did your
fathers not persecute? And they killed those
who foretold the coming of the Just One, of whom
you now have become the betrayers and murderers."

....

They had heard enough. The Sanhedrin, showing an enormous surge of emotion, decided that the best way to deal with this troublemaker would be to execute him.

The Execution

> 54. When they heard these things they were cut to the heart,... 55. But he, being full of the Holy Spirit,...
> 56. and said, "Look! I see the heavens opened and the Son of Man standing at the right hand of God!"
> 58. and they cast him out of the city and stoned him....

For all the difference it makes, this was an illegal execution. As in the case of Jesus, they would have been required to go to the Roman officers before taking such action, for only the Romans could serve the death penalty. Thus, it would not be inaccurate to label this precipitous action as murder. It had all the legal backing of a mob lynching.

The trigger for violence was not Stephen's rebuke or even calling them **stiff-necked and uncircumcised in heart and ears!** It was Stephen saying, **"Look! I see the heavens opened and the Son of Man standing at the right hand of God!"** As Ernst Haenchen says, "If Jesus stands on the right hand of God, this must show that the Christians are right in the sight of God and that the High Council is virtually God's enemy."[3] From this point on, there was no stopping them.

Stephen died for his Lord with words similar to his Master's on his lips:

> 60. ..."Lord, do not charge them with this sin."...

Why was Stephen murdered?

Because this event is such a crucial turning point in the history of Christianity, let me concisely summarize what happened. Stephen had established that there was a fundamental, not just a superficial, difference between the old order, that of Jewish temple worship, and the new order, later called Christianity. No compromise was possible. All people groups, not just the Jews, could now have direct access to God through Jesus the Messiah. Gentiles could now be saved and remain Gentiles. This principle is the indispensable premise of all cross-cultural missionary work. It was, and still is, very difficult for many devout Jews to accept.

Stephen had made explicit what had always been implicit, and by doing it he had polarized the opinions. From that point on, high-level persecution was inevitable.

Luke Introduces Saul

58. ...And the witnesses laid down their clothes at the feet of a young man named Saul. 8:1. Now Saul was consenting to his death.... 3. As for Saul, he made havoc of the church, entering every house, and dragging off men and women, committing them to prison.

No church leader at this point could possibly have believed that Saul of Tarsus, undoubtedly called by some "Saul the Terrible," would later be transformed by the power of the Holy Spirit, and as the famous apostle Paul lead the advance of the kingdom of God into the Gentile world. It sounds very much as if he could have been the ringleader of the fierce persecution that began with Stephen's death.

Getting Rid of the Hellenistic Believers
Acts 8

....

1. ...At that time a great persecution arose against the church which was at Jerusalem; and they were all scattered throughout the regions of Judea and Samaria, except the apostles. 4. Therefore those who were scattered went everywhere preaching the word.

....

A chain reaction occurred. The more the Jews thought about the implications of Stephen's message, the more threatened they became. Previously, the persecutions had been directed specifically against the leaders such as Peter and John (see Acts 4:3), the 12 apostles (see Acts 5:18) or Stephen. Now, the fury of the enemies of the gospel is loosed against the believers in general for the first time.

In order to get an accurate picture, we should not interpret the phrase **they were all scattered** too literally. Everett Harrison warns us, "This can hardly be taken strictly, since many were detained and imprisoned. This is an example of hyperbole which is not uncommon in Scripture when emphasis is desired."[4] As an obvious example, Harrison points to Mark 1:5, which says that when John the Baptist came, "all the land of Judea" went out to him and "all" were baptized.

The three words **except the apostles** have more significance than many realize. The apostles, as far as we know, had not been personally involved in the incident with Stephen. They likely regarded it as a situation brought on by the Hellenistic group, which they had blessed by laying hands on the seven leaders, but for which they no longer felt a paternal responsibility. This is a common attitude of missionaries today who release the national church to their indigenous leadership, then distance themselves when the nationals make choices that may seem misguided to the missionaries. F. F. Bruce says, "We may conclude that it was the Hellenists in the church (the group in which Stephen had been a leader) who formed the main target of attack, and that it was they for the most part who were compelled to leave Jerusalem."[5] Then Bruce adds, "From this time onward the Jerusalem church appears to have been a predominantly 'Hebrew' body."[6]

Not that there were no exceptions, or that things would never change as time went on. We know, for example, that the person the Jerusalem church chose to make a fact-finding visit to Antioch about 15 years later was Barnabas, a Hellenistic disciple (see Acts 11:22).

The upshot of all of this?

---

4. Therefore those who were scattered went everywhere preaching the word.

As frequently happens, what seems at first glance to be a setback for the church is used by God for His glory and the spread of His kingdom.

Preaching Christ in Samaria

Stephen and Philip were the two highest-profile individuals among the seven chosen to lead the Hellenistic segment of the Jerusalem church. Stephen had been executed, and it is a safe assumption that the other six would have been included among those who fell victim to the great persecution in which they were all scattered throughout the regions of Judea and Samaria. Philip was one of those who went from Jerusalem to Samaria.

The late Stephen had been the theoretician between the two, developing the missiological and theological rationale for the possibility of church planting among the Samaritans. He had cleared the way for the notion of such a thing as a Samaritan disciple of Jesus, when previously there had only been *Jewish* disciples of Jesus. This sounds obvious to us today. But we have to be reminded that when Philip went to Samaria, probably the majority of Jewish believers, if approached in an opinion poll, would have said that Samaritans should only be allowed to become disciples of Jesus if they first agreed to become Jewish proselytes.

---

5. Then Philip went down to the city of Samaria and preached Christ to them. 6. And the multitudes with one accord heeded the things spoken by Philip, hearing and seeing the miracles which he did. 7. For unclean spirits, crying with a loud voice, came out of many who were possessed; and many who were paralyzed and lame were healed.

There are two important Philips in the New Testament. One, who was numbered among the original 12, was a Hebrew who had remained in Jerusalem. The other, a Hellenist, became Christianity's first recognized cross-cultural missionary, called of God to evangelize Samaria.

We hear a good deal today about evangelists such as Billy Graham or Luis Palau. It is interesting that the only example we have in the New Testament of a person who was specifically recognized as an evangelist was Philip. Much later in the book of Acts he is referred to as **Philip the evangelist, and he had four virgin daughters who prophesied** (Acts 21:8,9).

Philip, presumably, had at least two dominant spiritual gifts, that of evangelist and the gift of missionary. We do not know whether his colleague, Stephen, had either of these gifts, but Stephen obviously had the gift of wisdom (see Acts 6:10) and of faith (see Acts 6:5). My definitions of Philip's gifts are as follows:

> The gift of *evangelist* is the special ability that God gives to certain members of the Body of Christ to share the gospel with unbelievers in such a way that men and women become Jesus' disciples and responsible members of the Body of Christ.[7]

> The gift of *missionary* is the special ability that God gives to certain members of the Body of Christ to minister whatever other spiritual gifts they have in a second culture.[8]

Most evangelists we know are monocultural evangelists, but Philip is the prototype of subsequent cross-cultural evangelists. His target was Samaria, although we do not know whether this meant the city of Samaria itself or the region of Samaria. Some speculate that the city of Samaria, where he first preached, might have been Gitta, which was the hometown of Simon the sorcerer, who appears later.

Evangelizing by Word and Deed

Philip's ministry had two parallel and closely related elements: word and deed. We read of **the things spoken by Philip** and also of **the miracles which he did.** This follows what would have been expected from Jesus' words in Acts 1:8, where He spoke of receiving the power of the Holy Spirit and also of being cross-cultural witnesses. Philip was practicing New Testament "power evangelism," to borrow the title of John Wimber's seminal book on the subject.[9] Because this is the only biblical description we have of the ministry of a person specifically designated as an "evangelist," one wonders why more people today would not seek to combine miraculous deeds with their words, as did Philip. If they did, we might also see similar **multitudes with one accord** responding to such a holistic gospel. Fortunately, the number who are now combining the two is increasing dramatically around the world, and the kingdom of God has never been spreading more rapidly.

Philip's ministry in word was **[preaching] Christ to them.** This means he was presenting Jesus as Messiah, a synonym of Christ. This message made sense to the Samaritans, as we know from the Samaritan woman whom Jesus met at the well. She said, "I know that Messiah is coming" (who is called Christ). "When He comes, He will tell us all things" (John 4:25). Philip's goal was to see large numbers of "Messianic Samaritans," and, from what we read here, he was accomplishing it well.

The major reason people in Samaria would listen to his claims that Jesus was the long-awaited Messiah was the power ministry seen through miracles, healings and deliverance from evil spirits. I would imagine that Philip also had the spiritual gifts of healing, miracles and deliverance to accompany his gifts of evangelist and missionary.

It is notable that Luke would mention that the Samaritan multitudes were **hearing and seeing the miracles which he did.** It is unusual to think of "hearing" miracles until Luke goes on to say: **For unclean spirits, crying with a loud voice, came out of many.** These evangelistic meetings, apparently, were noisy, rather boisterous and probably messy events. Incorporating mass deliverance into evangelistic crusades is not part of the usual experience of most American Christians, but it is as common in many Third World settings today as it was in Samaria then.

I think, for example, of Argentine evangelist Carlos Anna-
condia, a personal friend of mine, who could hardly conceive of
public evangelism apart from demonic deliverance. I have been
among the thousands standing in the open air in his meetings
when he forcefully rebukes, even taunts, the demonic spirits in
the audience. Scores, sometimes hundreds, fall to the ground
under demonic manifestations with many of the demons crying
with a loud voice. Well-trained teams of "stretcher bearers" cir-
culate through the crowd, escorting or physically carrying the
demonized to a huge tent behind the platform called the "spiritual intensive care unit." There, skilled deliverance teams minister
one by one, sometimes through the night, until all have been
freed from the dark angels who had been oppressing them.

I mention this to keep us from thinking that such noisy and
messy, but at the same time powerful, works of the Holy Spirit are
simply relics of the past. They are also happening today where
the kingdom of God is in rapid advance.

What Good Are Miracles and Signs?

Ministries of the miraculous, where paralyzed people walk, deaf
people hear and demonized people are freed, never saved anyone.
Healings bring glory to God, but even the most dramatic ones are
at best temporal. They do not impart eternal life. The *deeds* only
prepare the way for the *Word*.

But, make no mistake, they prepare the way well. The whole
Gospel of John is organized around seven miracles (changing
water to wine, healing a boy, healing a cripple, feeding 5,000,
walking on water, healing a blind man and raising a dead man),
and as John says, "Jesus did many other signs" (John 20:30). John
tells us that the seven signs he did choose to include in his
Gospel "are written that you may believe that Jesus is the Christ,
the Son of God, and that believing you may have life in His

name" (John 20:31). The miracles themselves draw attention, but they are only signs pointing to salvation through faith in Jesus as Messiah. This is what Philip was practicing.

Results of Philip's Power Evangelism

....

> 8. And there was great joy in that city. 12. But when they believed Philip as he preached the things concerning the kingdom of God and the name of Jesus Christ, both men and women were baptized. 14. Now when the apostles who were at Jerusalem heard that Samaria had received the word of God, they sent Peter and John to them, 25. So when they had testified and preached the word of the Lord, they returned to Jerusalem, preaching the gospel in many villages of the Samaritans.

....

There was great joy in the city of Samaria from the outset of Philip's ministry there. At this point, it was probably not as yet the joy of salvation, but the joy over being healed and seeing their loved ones healed. Whatever Philip had come to say was "good news," another term for the gospel.

Many then believed. They believed the good news concerning the kingdom of God that Philip had been demonstrating before their very eyes. The Kingdom had come, and Samaritans were being accepted into it. They sealed their commitment through public baptism, and the Church of Jesus Christ was firmly plant-ed in their midst.

When this news got back to the Hebrew believers who had remained in Jerusalem after the persecution of the Hellenists, it must have caused no small stir. They had not sent Philip as a missionary—he had been driven out by the Jews, probably at the instigation of Saul of Tarsus. How much attention they had paid to Stephen's historic message we do not know, but, in any case, the phenomenon of large numbers of Messianic Samaritans must have caused the Hebrew believers an uncomfortable mixture of joy and consternation.

The fact that they sent their two top leaders, Peter and John, to investigate, indicates that the issues must have been seen as extraordinarily significant. These Samaritans were being baptized in the name of Jesus. Were they really brothers and sisters in Christ? Peter and John had both been with Jesus at Sychar in Samaria when "many of the Samaritans of that city believed in Him," hearing the testimony of the woman at the well (see John 4:39-42). They had been prepared. Peter also had been the representative of the 12 for receiving the keys of the Kingdom of heaven (see Matt. 16:18,19), and, as such, he was present when the Kingdom opened wide to the Jews on Pentecost (see Acts 2), and he was here when it opened to the Samaritans, and later when it opened to the Gentiles in the house of Cornelius (see Acts 10).

The Samaritans Received the Holy Spirit

....

14. ...they sent Peter and John to them, 15. who, when
they had come down, prayed for them that they might
receive the Holy Spirit. 16. For as yet He had fallen upon
none of them. They had only been baptized in the name of
the Lord Jesus. 17. Then they laid hands on them, and
they received the Holy Spirit.

....

Acts 8:14-17 is a favorite text for those who teach that the baptism in the Holy Spirit is a second work of God's grace subsequent to salvation. The Samaritans had been saved and baptized in water but had not as yet received the Holy Spirit. Through prayer and the laying on of hands, the Holy Spirit came upon them.

Others disagree. The reason this has become a continuing debate among committed Christians is that the Bible itself is not clear. Passages such as this one encourage one point of view. Passages such as 1 Corinthians 12:13, "For by one Spirit we were all baptized into one body...and have all been made to drink into one Spirit," encourage the point of view that the baptism of the Holy Spirit occurs at conversion. Subsequent to conversion, many fillings with the Holy Spirit or special anointings, or whatever, can occur. I have my personal point of view, but I am not interested here to attempt to prove that I am right and that others are wrong. Fortunately, we are all seeking the same thing, namely, the powerful energizing of the Holy Spirit for ministry.

I will, however, reiterate what I mentioned in chapter 4 about the three phases of the Pentecost event. I believe that Pentecost, or the coming of the Holy Spirit, was a one-time historical incident, as were the death and resurrection of Jesus. This unique first-century event had three parts or phases. Phase one happened on the Day of Pentecost itself in Acts 2; phase two happened here in Acts 8; and phase three happened later in the house of Cornelius in Acts 10. My point is that if the Pentecost event in three parts was a unique historical occurrence, there is no intrinsic need to suppose that the sequence of first being saved, then later receiving the Holy Spirit, would necessarily carry on in the Church through the centuries.

It seems strange that Luke mentions speaking in tongues in phases one and three, but not here in phase two. Still, the apostles must have had some tangible way of knowing that when **they laid hands on them...they received the Holy Spirit.** There is no denying that speaking in tongues is one of the biblical evidences of being filled with the Holy Spirit, but I do not agree that it is the one and only validating physical evidence.

A milestone in this century-long debate was the recent publication of *The Beauty of Spiritual Language* by Jack Hayford, one of the most impeccably credentialed, classical Pentecostal leaders of our times. Classical Pentecostals form the largest bloc of those who have historically argued for the "initial evidence" doctrine that all who receive the baptism of the Holy Spirit validate that experience physically by speaking in tongues at least once.

In his book, which strongly encourages the gift of tongues for all Christians, Hayford says: "As readily as I want to honor my Pentecostal forebears for preserving the testimony of tongues and for generating a passion for Spirit-fullness among millions, at the same time I confess that I believe an unintentional but nonetheless restrictive barrier was built," referring to the initial-evidence requirement.[10]

Although speaking in tongues can be an evidence, and quite possibly was in Samaria, other evidences can be new intimacy with the Father, the joy of the Holy Spirit, falling in the power of God, power to heal the sick and cast out demons, prophecy, a passion for winning the lost and many others.

The Apostles' Verdict

The missiological question remains: How did the Hebrew apostles, Peter and John, like what they saw in Samaria? Could they accept the radical shift involved in affirming the validity of "Messianic Samaritans"? Could Samaritans become part of the family of Jehovah God without first becoming Jews? Apparently they were convinced because:

....

25. ...they returned to Jerusalem, preaching the gospel in many villages of the Samaritans.

....

Peter and John were evangelizing Samaritans, planting churches in Samaritan villages and not requiring them to switch their place of contact with God from Mount Gerazim to Jerusalem. This would have been a difficult adjustment for Jews to make, but the Samaritans were at least half Jews. Considerably more difficult would be the adjustment they would have to make in the future when they would cross the barrier to the Gentiles.

Simon the Sorcerer and Spiritual Warfare

A very important incident occurs when Philip is in Samaria, which has implications far beyond cross-cultural church planting in Samaria itself. Almost half of the Samaria passage explains Philip's ministry to just one individual, Simon the Sorcerer, and the help he then received from Peter. I say it has wider implications because it is the first time Luke discusses an event involving occult-level spiritual warfare.

Three levels of spiritual warfare may be fairly clearly discerned, all of them relating to each other through the intricate workings of the kingdom of darkness: (1) ground-level spiritual warfare that is casting ordinary demons out of people; (2) occult-level spiritual warfare involving the satanic power of magicians, sorcerers, witches, New Age channelers, shamans and the like; and (3) strategic-level spiritual warfare dealing with principalities, powers and territorial spirits.

The intrusion of the kingdom of God into previously unchallenged areas dominated by the kingdom of Satan is an underlying theme throughout Acts, although Luke surfaces it only from time to time. Yale University biblical scholar, Susan Garrett, has recently produced what I would imagine is the definitive study of magic and the demonic in Luke's writings, *The Demise of the Devil*. In her book, she says, "The remarks about Satan in Luke's Gospel and Acts are, if small in quantity, mammoth in significance. When taken seriously, the traces and clues that Luke has dropped along the way suggest that one can scarcely overestimate Satan's importance in the history of Salvation told by Luke."[11]

To mention some of these "traces and clues," ground-level spiritual warfare is described frequently throughout Acts. Another example of occult-level spiritual warfare comes with the seven sons of Sceva in Acts 19. Strategic-level spiritual warfare surfaces with Bar-Jesus or Elymas in Acts 13 and with the Python spirit in Acts 16, and all three are tied in with Paul's ministry in Ephesus in Acts 19.

Here in Samaria the statement that **unclean spirits, crying with a loud voice, came out of many who were possessed (8:7)** displays ground-level spiritual warfare. The occult-level warfare involves Simon the Sorcerer:

> **9.** But there was a certain man called Simon, who previously practiced sorcery in the city and astonished the people of Samaria, claiming that he was someone great,
> **10.** to whom they all gave heed, from the least to the greatest, saying, "This man is the great power of God."
> **11.** And they heeded him because he had astonished them with his sorceries for a long time. **13.** Then Simon himself also believed; and when he was baptized he continued with Philip, and was amazed, seeing the miracles and signs which were done.
>
> **18.** Now when Simon saw that through the laying on of the apostles' hands the Holy Spirit was given, he offered them money, **19.** saying, "Give me

this power also, that anyone on whom I lay hands may receive the Holy Spirit." 20. But Peter said to him, "Your money perish with you, because you thought that the gift of God could be purchased with money! 21. You have neither part nor portion in this matter, for your heart is not right in the sight of God. 22. Repent therefore of this your wickedness, and pray God if perhaps the thought of your heart may be forgiven you. 23. For I see that you are poisoned by bitterness and bound by iniquity."

24. Then Simon answered and said, "Pray to the Lord for me, that none of the things which you have spoken may come upon me."

This story contains many unknowns. Was Simon's original profession of faith and baptism valid or just a sham? After Peter later rebuked him, did he repent? As far as Simon the Sorcerer is concerned, does the story have a happy ending or a sad ending? Although I have no way of proving it, I would like to believe that Simon was really saved through Philip's preaching, that he subsequently made a huge mistake as a new babe in Christ, that the Holy Spirit used Peter's rebuke to straighten him out, and that he repented and lived happily ever after. Whether this is the actual case or not, what do we learn from this incident?

What Can We Learn?

Simon the Sorcerer's power in the city was enormous. The citizens all gave heed to this man **from the least to the greatest,** and they regarded him as God, **saying, "This man is the great power of God."** It could well be that the territorial spirit assigned to keep this city in darkness had attached itself to the Sorcerer. Underneath the whole thing we should recognize, as Susan

Garrett says, that these "narrated encounters are not merely skirmishes between prophets or wonder-workers, but confrontations between Satan and the Spirit of God."[12] In order to gain this power over the city, Simon's magical power must have been real. "Simon is no mere con artist, or cheap charlatan," says Garrett, "but someone far more sinister, endowed with the power of Satan and disguising himself as the 'great power of God.'"[13]

Philip came into that city, which was under a fascination of power, and most Samaritans probably not even realizing the power to which they were subject was the power of Satan. The only kind of message that could possibly have impressed these people was a message involving not only a word, but also a demonstration of power. Missiologists call it a "power encounter." Missiologist Paul Pierson says, "The message was authenticated by clashes between the healing power of God and the destructive forces of evil....Such 'power encounters' would often accompany new breakthroughs in the Book of Acts and all through Christian history."[14] Philip's miracles and signs, done under the authentic power of God, were clearly recognized as superior to the counterfeit power of the devil. Even Simon the Sorcerer was amazed, **seeing the miracles and signs which were done.**

Luke is showing us here that Philip's message was an early reflection of Jesus' later assignment to the apostle Paul. Paul was to go to the nations **to open their eyes and to turn them from darkness to light, and from the power of Satan to God** (Acts 26:18). Susan Garrett says, "Philip's dramatic exorcisms and healings of the possessed, paralyzed, and lame gave incontrovertible proof of Satan's subjugation, and hence of the certainty of the Kingdom of God with Christ as Lord."[15]

Philip's power ministry was the beachhead in this intense episode of spiritual warfare. The decisive victory, as far as the city was concerned, was Peter's rebuke to the powers of darkness operating through Simon the Sorcerer. Satan's last stand was to tempt Simon to offer money to buy God's power. This would have been normal behavior among professional magicians and sorcerers, so it was an easy temptation for Simon to yield to. Although Peter doesn't address Satan or the spirits directly, his rebuke to Simon is a public announcement that God's power is demonstrably greater than Satan's. The **bitterness and iniquity** that had poisoned Simon was from the prince of evil.

Susan Garrett brilliantly expresses the essence of the historic power encounter: "Satan does still have some power, but he is handily subjugated when confronted by the vastly greater divine authority that Christians wield. Peter's righteous rebuke reduces Simon from a famous magician, impiously acclaimed by all the people of Samaria as 'the great power of God,' to a meek man who fears for his own destruction and so asks the servant of the Lord to intercede for him."[16]

South to Ethiopia and North to Caesarea

As a further demonstration of the extraordinary power of God on Philip for cross-cultural evangelism, no less than an angel comes to Philip and instructs him to go to the Gaza Strip. Afterward, an even more remarkable miracle occurs when Philip is bodily transported by the Holy Spirit from there to Azotus (or Ashdod [8:39,40]).

26. Now an angel of the Lord spoke to Philip, saying, "Arise and go toward the south along the road which goes down from Jerusalem to Gaza."... 27. So he arose and went. And behold, a man of Ethiopia, a eunuch of great authority under Candace the queen of the Ethiopians, who had charge of all her treasury, and had come to Jerusalem to worship, 28. was returning.... 35. Then Philip opened

his mouth, and beginning at this Scripture, preached Jesus
to him. 37. ...And he [the eunuch] answered and said, "I
believe that Jesus Christ is the Son of God." 38. ...And
both Philip and the eunuch went down into the water,
and he baptized him.

Although Luke does not tell us for sure, there is a strong possibility that this Ethiopian was a Gentile God-fearer like
Cornelius. These God-fearers were born Gentiles who worshiped
Jehovah God but who had not taken the more radical step of
becoming Jewish proselytes. If so, it is the first instance we have
of a Gentile conversion, but because Luke leaves it rather
ambiguous and makes nothing more of it, we will also postpone
the discussion of E-3 Gentile evangelism until we come to Acts
10, where Peter visits the house of Cornelius.

From there, Philip preaches the gospel up the eastern coast of
the Mediterranean, and the story of how the gospel first moved
from Jerusalem and Judea to Samaria ends. Next, the kingdom of
God pushes on through many of the gates of Hades, which try to
hinder it, to the Gentiles, whom Jesus termed **the end of the
earth** (Acts 1:8).

Reflection Questions

1. Name some actual examples of E-1 and E-2 and E-3 evangelism in your own city or nation. What are the major differences in the planning and execution of each?
2. Something that Stephen said must have been extremely
   upsetting to his hearers, causing them to murder him. What
   exactly was it?
3. Who were the Samaritans? Why was evangelizing them not a
   normal thing to expect from Jews?

4. Do you think the Samaritans spoke in tongues when they received the Holy Spirit? Why?
5. Describe the differences between ground-level, occult-level and strategic-level spiritual warfare. Where does Simon the Sorcerer fit into the picture?

Notes

1. F. F. Bruce, *Commentary on the Book of Acts* (Grand Rapids, MI: William B. Eerdmans Publishing Co., 1988), p. 124. Used by permission.
2. Charles Van Engen, *God's Missionary People* (Grand Rapids, MI: Baker Book House Company, 1991), p. 26.
3. Ernst Haenchen, *The Acts of the Apostles: A Commentary* (Louisville, KY: Westminster Press, 1971), p. 295.
4. Everett F. Harrison, *Acts: The Expanding Church* (Chicago, IL: Moody Press, 1975), pp. 129-130.
5. Bruce, *Commentary*, p. 162.
6. Ibid.
7. C. Peter Wagner, *Your Spiritual Gifts Can Help Your Church Grow* (Ventura, CA: Regal Books, 1994), p. 157.
8. Ibid., p. 179.
9. John Wimber and Kevin Springer, *Power Evangelism* (San Francisco, CA: HarperSanFrancisco, 1985, 1992).
10. Jack Hayford, *The Beauty of Spiritual Language* (Dallas, TX: Word Inc., 1992), p. 92.
11. Reprinted by permission from THE DEMISE OF THE DEVIL by Susan Garrett, copyright © 1989 Augsburg Fortress, p. 37.
12. Garrett, *Demise*, p. 75.
13. Ibid.
14. Paul E. Pierson, *Themes from Acts* (Ventura, CA: Regal Books, 1982), p. 67. Used by permission.
15. Garrett, *Demise*, p. 65.
16. Ibid., p. 74.

INDEX

··

···

···